Angus Campbell (1939–2015) was a linguist, translator and scholar. After a long career as an international advertising executive, he retired to Sicily where he was resident for many years. He was an expert in the political, diplomatic, social and cultural history of eighteenth-century Sicily and his interest in Domenico Caracciolo was borne out of that research.

'This is the first work in English to be devoted to an important figure in the history of Enlightenment Europe. Caracciolo is brought alive through his colourful correspondence, only available before in Italian.'

William Doyle,
Emeritus Professor of History,
University of Bristol

Portrait of Domenico Caracciolo, courtesy of the Fondazione
Federico Secondo, Palermo.

ANGUS CAMPBELL

SICILY AND THE ENLIGHTENMENT

The World of *Domenico Caracciolo,* *Thinker* and *Reformer*

I.B. TAURIS

LONDON · NEW YORK

Published in 2016 by
I.B.Tauris & Co. Ltd
London • New York
www.ibtauris.com

ISBN: 978 1 78453 575 9
eISBN: 978 0 85772 899 9
ePDF: 978 0 85772 802 9

A full CIP record for this book is available from the British Library
A full CIP record is available from the Library of Congress

Library of Congress Catalog Card Number: available

Typeset by Saxon Graphics Ltd, Derby
Printed and bound by CPI Group (UK) Ltd, Croydon, CR0 4YY

MIX
Paper from
responsible sources
FSC
www.fsc.org   FSC® C013604

Contents

Foreword   vii

Part One   DIPLOMAT (*Allegro con spirito*)
  1 Beginnings   3
  2 Turin   11
  3 London   23
  4 Paris   45

Part Two   INTERMEZZO
  5 Why was Caracciolo the Choice?   63
  6 What Awaited Him   71

Part Three   VICEROY (*Vivace assai*)
  7 Settling In   101
  8 The Abolition of the Inquisition   115
  9 Clearing the Decks   125
 10 Broadside   143
 11 Picking Up   167

Part Four   PRIME MINISTER (*Andante sostenuto*)
 12 Naples at Last   185

Conclusion   203

Notes   206
Bibliography   219
Index   222

Foreword

Angus Campbell (1939–2015) was a linguist, translator and scholar. After studying medieval history at Magdalen College, Oxford, he spent several years in the small town of Oristano in Sardinia teaching English. He then returned to London and embarked on a career in advertising. In 1969 he married Caterina Mollica, a Sicilian, and they moved to Rome where he continued in advertising, eventually setting up his own company. There they lived in a rented flat near the Spanish Steps, with the famous Caffè Greco behind them and the equally famous restaurant Ranieri opposite their front door and the rooftop flag of the Knights of Malta fluttering right in front of their balcony. From there they moved to their own flat nearby in the Via Vittoria, where their rooftop terrace overlooked the gardens of the Greek Convent.

The Mollicas are a large and distinguished Sicilian family and, after retiring at the beginning of the new millennium, the Campbell-Mollicas moved from Rome to the family compound near Calatafimi in western Sicily. From there the great tourist site of Segesta is visible a few kilometres away and a swim in its hot thermal pool became part of Campbell's daily routine. They lived first in a small cottage and later in the big house nearby, which they had converted from the ruins of an old farmhouse. In Calatafimi, as in Rome, they played host to a stream of friends and every autumn to the olive pickers who would come from all over the world to pick their olives in exchange for board and lodging.

Their life there elicited from Campbell his first book, *Calatafimi: Behind the Stone Walls of a Sicilian Town* (2008), a book full of the humorous details of local life interspersed with bursts of history, and overall a loving tribute to his wife's family. In his last years, Campbell managed to complete his final book on the much more familiar subject of Samuel Butler and his links with Sicily. He was stoical in pain, finally succumbing to cancer on 2 November 2015. His widow has laid his ashes to rest in their beautiful garden where she, their children and grandchildren can continue to keep him abreast of all the local gossip.

Fred Atapour, September 2016

Part One

Diplomat

Allegro con spirito

1

Beginnings

※❀※

D omenico Caracciolo was born in Spain in 1715. His father, Tommaso Caracciolo, Marchese di Villamaina e Capriglia and of an old noble Neapolitan family, was serving in His Catholic Majesty's Army; his mother, D. Maria de Alcantara Porras y Silva, was Spanish.

Very little is known of Domenico's early life. He and his family returned to Naples, where he received his education and his formation as a young man, when he was still a child. After an unsatisfying career as a magistrate, he left the city at the age of 37, returning at the age of 71 as prime minister. The intervening years were taken up with diplomatic posts in Turin, London and Paris, and, most significantly, as viceroy in Sicily from 1781 to 1786, where he battled to impose rational reforms on what was then the backward feudal corner of 'Enlightened' Europe.

That he was a younger son marked Domenico's life in various ways. In the first place, it meant that, though he would never be forbidden from marrying, he would be unlikely to make a brilliant match – efforts in that matter would be reserved for his elder brother. He resolved his own sentimental life in a most rational eighteenth-century way by picking and choosing discreetly, often among ladies of the theatre, as he went through life. When asked once by Louis XV about his love life, he replied to His Majesty that he bought it ready made,[1] though usually his references to lady friends in letters were far less revealing. What this means to a biographer, however, is that he did not have a stable home in the normal sense of the word. There was no wife and children, no in-laws, no family estate, all of which engender documents, arguments and stories, and therefore Caracciolo's private life is more difficult to track.

Not being the eldest son also meant that he did not inherit. Although his family was old and noble, it was not at this time affluent, and Domenico (Mimmo to his friends) had found that some form of a career was expedient. In his station of life there were only three possibilities: the army, the church or the law. The latter two offered eventual outlets into diplomacy and politics. As we shall see, his own education, as well, probably, as popular anticlerical feeling in Naples at the time, were to exclude the church as a possibility. But this is to jump ahead in time. What needs to be emphasised is that his being single and becoming a man of office means that we have to unravel his life by means of official letters, decrees and hearsay.

Despite energetic efforts by eminent Neapolitan historians, very little is known about Caracciolo's early life in Naples. Benedetto Croce[2] has a delightful picture, which might well be true, of Domenico and other young members of his family being taught in a sort of extended-family college, and goes on to say that he studied music, poetry and mathematics, presumably at the same school, but no hard evidence is offered. In later years, however, Caracciolo fought bravely in Paris in favour of the Italian musician Piccinni against the court-favoured Gluck, tried hard to inveigle the French mathematician Le Grange to teach at the University of Palermo, showed energetic interest in all forms of literature (which involved him in bookish activities that ranged from being intimately concerned with the consequences of Alfieri's duel in London to promoting Arabic studies in Sicily), and was also involved in the importation of foreign books that, for reasons of censure, were not to be had in the kingdom. It is fair to assume, then, that his schooling was soundly based wherever and however it was carried out.

All available sources are agreed that two leading Neapolitan intellectuals were particularly important to the young Caracciolo in these formative years: the economist, philosopher and moralist Genovesi; and the anticlerical philosopher Giannone. Genovesi, who began public teaching in 1749 three years before Caracciolo left Naples and was appointed to the first university chair in economics in Europe in 1754 at Naples' Federico II University, aimed in his teaching at the destruction of what remained of mediaeval institutions and mentality, the elimination of the abuses of the privileged classes, and the construction of a more equitable and reasonable society. He was also an active reformer in the field of secondary education. Giannone was concerned that abuses of the church and the papacy were impeding the natural development of the country, which ought naturally to look to the state for social justice; he died while imprisoned for his anti-religious stance.

By the time Caracciolo was preparing to enter the magistrature, Genovesi's and Giannone's teachings were beginning to create ripples in public opinion. It was, in a much simplified nutshell, that the state was not the king backed up by the barons and the church, but a lay institution, independent of all other powers, integral and co-interested with the people and with clear duties towards the people. Genovesi's and Giannone's thinking was more sophisticated than that stark synopsis and was studied with conviction by the young Caracciolo and his peers: their teachings, particularly those of Genovesi, remained in Caracciolo's mind for the rest of his life and motivated most of his subsequent reforms in Sicily, though it must be emphasised that he was a convinced believer in the institution of monarchy and what is now known as Enlightened despotism.

Caracciolo's social position limited the choice of his career. Although his father had served as a soldier and he himself recorded his appreciation of the role of the aristocracy in the army, particularly in his correspondence with his minister Tanucci while serving as a diplomat in Turin, Caracciolo did not choose the army as a career. This whittled his choice down to the law, as his schooling and convictions obviously eliminated the church. However, he was faced with a further serious problem that was to trouble him throughout life: he was either born or became an idealist. It was inevitable that the legal system operating in eighteenth-century Naples would sorely delude him. He chose to become a judge in the court of the *Vicaria*, a 'low' court avoided by the lawyers who despised the career of judge[3] (the career he had embarked on and which he himself did not, in fact, appreciate), and thoroughly hated it. He talked with hatred of lawyers and courts ever afterwards (though later, compared with Sicilian courts, the Neapolitan courts actually got off lighter). Because he knew the ins and outs of the system, his criticisms were very telling. Caracciolo had learned to despise the theoretical wrongs of social injustice from the teachings of Genovesi, and now he came face to face with them and the system that manipulated them; in addition, he had to listen to the squabbling and shouting that accompanied legal proceedings, of which he complained so often afterwards.

Caracciolo found himself at odds with the society in which he lived and felt the need to get away from Naples. Something of what he felt can be gleaned from a phrase in a letter from London to his famous Neapolitan friend, the wit Abbé Galiani, in Paris, concerning his nephews. It is dated much later than his time in Naples, 28 August 1770, but clearly harks back to it:

> I do not think of going back home for the moment. However
> soon I shall have to ask for leave for a few months on account

of my nephews. I wish to arrange a good education for them; and perhaps to extricate them, to separate them forever from the mass of scoundrels (*Lazzarismo*) and corruption that surround them there, I want to bring them up in a college in Paris where I can keep an eye on them.[4]

Throughout his life he was interested in education.

Whatever Caracciolo's personal reactions to the capital of the Kingdom of the Two Sicilies (Naples and Sicily), one should not lose sight of the fact that Naples was a major European city, and that King Charles (before moving on to become Charles III of Spain) and his chief minister Tanucci had done a great deal towards reforming the kingdom. Much had been achieved in the fields of law, public works, industry, agriculture, the arts, the church and trade by the middle of the century, though there was an enormous amount that still needed doing. But there is no doubt that the king and his minister could lay claim to be considered among the minor Enlightened absolutists. Despite Caracciolo's experiences in what he considered more Enlightened climes after he left Naples, there was always the feeling, when he was struggling with reforms in Sicily, that perhaps Naples was better at solving problems.

He was saved from Neapolitan misery when his abilities were recognised by Marquis Fogliani, the then prime minister (or by the '*Gobba*', or the 'Hunchback', his wife, according to Tanucci, his successor as the principal minister), who picked Caracciolo out for a delicate diplomatic mission in 1752. This was a great liberation for him, both from a career that could not accommodate his ideals and a society that did not measure up to his standards. His elder brother ceded the paternal title of Marchese as a suitable accompaniment for the new diplomat (retaining the grander, grandmaternal one of Duke of San Teodoro), and off Caracciolo set.

The Italy and Europe that awaited him was very unsettled. The 1748 Treaty of Aix-la-Chapelle had satisfied nobody, as the outbreak of the Seven Years' War eight years later suggests. Caracciolo's kingdom was still a regency, with the principal minister Tanucci reporting directly to Charles III of Spain (King Ferdinand did not come of age until 1767), and, with the exception of Rome, the rest of Italy was as ever very much under the influence of either Austria or Savoy (also known as the Kingdom of Sardinia). Elsewhere, Austria was plotting ways of retrieving Silesia from Prussia; the English and the French were vying with each other in distant parts of the globe; Spain was mostly concerned with South America. Prussia had its eyes on the Baltic and Russia had its on Prussia, and Savoy was waiting to pick up any little bit of new territory that came its way, especially Milan. People of Caracciolo's class, inclination and education would have been aware of this general political situation; Caracciolo would also have been aware of the European cultural condition, given his early studies of Genovesi and Giannone. He would not have left Naples *naïf*, but he would also have been aware that he had a great deal to learn.

From this point onwards until he finally disembarked at Palermo to take up his appointment as Viceroy of Sicily, his correspondence, and particularly his official correspondence, was packed with the experience he gained in his travels, which he transformed into lessons to be learnt by the Two Sicilies. This included how the young aristocrats in Turin did military service, how equitably the taxes were divided among the social classes in Lombardy, what importance was paid to commerce in England, the equilibrium between the rich and the poor in France … these were veritable lectures mostly directed at Tanucci, who had taken over as chief minister in Naples, and was in fact continuing the programme of legal, ecclesiastical, economic and administrative reforms that went some way towards righting a few of the wrongs that had struck the young Caracciolo. Little of note, however, was attempted in Sicily for constitutional reasons.

Caracciolo's epistolary lectures began coming first from Turin, then from London and afterwards from Paris. They dealt with day-to-day matters apart from the advice, but his diplomatic duties were quite gentlemanly – trade disputes or treaties, positions as to wars, the searching of ships, fishing rights and so on – and Naples was not a large nor a belligerent power, but the advice continued. Its elements were fairly constant: social justice, trade, equitable taxation, parliamentary issues, freedom, the usefulness of a middle class, and the various realities that were becoming apparent in the new Europe of the mid-1700s.

2

Turin

❧❦❧

The secret mission for which King Charles III, through Naples' chief minister Fogliani, had chosen Caracciolo was indeed delicate.

After dealing with the Austrian succession and the ownership of Silesia, the Treaty of Aix-la-Chapelle went on to stipulate that the Duchy of Parma (duke of which Charles had been before becoming king in Naples) should be handed to Don Philip, the younger son of Philip V of Spain. Not only that: Don Philip should also succeed to the Kingdom of the Two Sicilies when Charles, Philip V's elder son and the incumbent king, eventually became king of Spain on the death of his half-brother Ferdinand. Charles refused to ratify this treaty, or a subsequent treaty between Austria, Spain and Sardinia signed at Aranjuez in 1752, which further guaranteed those terms. He quite naturally wanted his own children, not his younger brother, to inherit the Two Sicilies.

Caracciolo's secret mission was, with the utmost discretion, to sound out the opinions of various courts on this issue. These courts, it should be noted, were among the most important in Europe, yet Caracciolo, although already 37 years old, had absolutely no diplomatic experience. The question has to be asked: why Caracciolo? His biographer Francesco Brancato[1] suggests two reasons. First, he had in abundance the precise culture required of a diplomat at that time (it coincided, incidentally, with what he himself later prescribed in detail for his nephew, the Marquis Gallo, who was to become an important diplomat and politician[2]). Secondly, at this juncture, Naples was beginning to feel the need for independence from the Spanish throne and needed to build up its own diplomatic network.

So, feeling much elated at his new-found freedom from the drudgery of the law, Caracciolo left 'privately' in December 1752 with an itinerary that was to include the courts of Rome, Florence, Turin, Paris and Madrid.

When he came to be presented at court in Turin he managed to give vague answers to the pointed questions he was asked, but by the time he arrived at Versailles he was being asked when he was leaving for Madrid and was answering, unconvincingly, that he was not travelling on orders but for pleasure. What happened is not clear, but what he was up to had become public knowledge, and his mission was abruptly ended in Paris, from where Caracciolo penned a stream of desperate letters to Fogliani in Naples imploring him not to send him back to being a judge once more (a move that was actually being mooted). He wrote to Fogliani:

> Trusting in the protection and the goodwill that Your Excellency has to such a high degree shown in me ... I confess and declare that the great favour bestowed on me has shaken me deeply ... because I can clearly see that I am shortly destined to re-attach that barbarous chain to my foot which Your Excellency's powerful arm had liberated from it ... that cursed calling, the legal profession, so against my nature, my disposition ... I implore Your Excellency, as much as I can and know how, to keep firm for the career embarked on.[3]

Despite this far-from-auspicious beginning, Caracciolo was in luck, for this was a time of diplomatic movement. His 'delicate' mission had been cut short in Paris, but he was asked to stay on there. It so happened that the Neapolitan envoy in Turin was needed in London, and a position became vacant in the former. Fogliani gave Caracciolo a second chance.

King Charles, on the other hand, did not give Fogliani such a reprieve:

> his credit at Court beginning to vacillate, being contended by the Prince of Aragona and the Marquis of Squillace, and King Charles being displeased that he had been unable to rid him of the article in the Treaty of Aix-La-Chapelle [concerning the reversion of the Two Sicilies to Don Philip] he transferred [Fogliani] to be Viceroy of Sicily and gave the secretaryship of foreign affairs to the Marquis Tanucci.[4]

If nothing else, this shows that the king was greatly interested in the 'delicate mission', and did not, apparently, blame Caracciolo for its failure.

The House of Savoy, which ruled as kings of Sardinia in Turin, had succeeded in the first half of the eighteenth century in building up one of the most efficient political and military machines in Europe – albeit on a small scale – from a collection of disunited and backward territories. It had done this by changing sides, selling its support and being generally unpredictable, which led it to be looked on with some suspicion, especially by the Spanish and the Neapolitans. The Austrian Hapsburgs were accustomed to using Savoy as allies in Italy and the English had been subsidising Savoyan armies with their naval eyes already on the southern Mediterranean. The Savoy government worked well, the legal system too; the taxes paid for a well-run army and its diplomacy was vigilant. The church was kept in check, efficient inroads had been made into noble privileges, and industry and trade were being very successfully developed along mercantalist lines. It wasn't perfect, but the country was emergent and promising.

From the moment he arrived in Turin, Caracciolo pounced on everything happening around him, and reported back to Tanucci as if his minister could never have imagined the things that his newly installed diplomat had seen, nor could ever have conceived how they might be adapted for use 'at home'. It is striking that almost all of the themes present in his correspondence with Tanucci were those of his later reforms when he became viceroy in Sicily. Caracciolo's letters were full of advice on how to run the Kingdom of the Two Sicilies, which often and quite understandably got on the minister's nerves, but Caracciolo was seeing new ideas in action, discovering how other people solved problems, gathering facts, gaining experience and working out how what he saw could be applied at home. Consider, for example, the silk industry: during the eighteenth century, 'Piedmontese' became synonymous with high quality in equipment and products in the silk trade, so much so that Caracciolo had sent back not only numerous detailed reports to Naples for local consumption there, but craftsmen with the latest technology to help in transforming the Sicilian industry.[5]

Take another example: the *catasto*, the correct surveying and registration of land that could ensure that society would be taxed on an equitable basis, was to become Caracciolo's major crusade in Sicily, but it already occupied a prominent place in his thought. He wrote constantly to Tanucci on how this was carried out in the territories of the Kingdom of Sardinia (Turin), urging him to apply the processes in Naples.[6] Tanucci responded with diminishing patience. On 20 August 1763, for example, he sent Caracciolo a missive containing a lengthy history lesson, pointing out the adaptability of different measures to different countries: he had introduced *catasto* [to Naples, not Sicily] to force the ecclesiastics and the rich to pay taxes, but the government had introduced the reforms badly and not a great deal of revenue had been produced; however, the clergy had made payments and the nobles were henceforth not as immune as they had been beforehand. Again, on 10 September 1763, Tanucci responded to Caracciolo: 'Oh! What a panegyric on the *catasto* in your revered letter of the 7th ... I was the first to propose that *catasto* you are pushing at me and the first to repent it.' He argued that the rate of taxation Caracciolo was proposing (14 per cent) was far too high for the wealth of Neapolitan agriculture, adding that although there was some moral right in Caracciolo's case, there was little that could be done under the existing conditions in Naples. At this time, King Charles had succeeded to the throne of Spain, and his son, King Ferdinand, who was 13, was ruling by regency. Tanucci wrote yet again on 24 September 1763 to say that 14 per cent was not a rate that Neapolitan agriculture could maintain, ending with a survey of the economies of the rest of Europe in support of his theory. This was more a lecture from a wise old uncle explaining that Caracciolo could not squeeze too much out of the landed classes in a poor agriculturally based economy such as that of Naples. His experience, he added, had taught him that if you want to rule over good citizens you must keep them happy, plus the hypocrisy and abuse of the priests had reduced them to a state of backwardness that they might perhaps escape from in a couple of centuries' time. These letters contained little by way of the cut and thrust of day-to-day diplomacy, but leisurely unravel both of their personalities and political outlooks between such bits of business that needed to be done.

Caracciolo was also much impressed by the spirit of state that he found at Turin and was not slow to express his feeling to Tanucci.[7] On 12 May 1756 he wrote: 'It is extraordinary that the spirit of the Court vivifies and extends to all classes of persons: *mens agitat molem*.' Again, on 22 June 1761, he penned:

Men of other nations are so different in principles and physiognomies, but here appear to be made from the same mould ... the city is all Court, and the inhabitants all have some direct or indirect relationship with it, and so they communicate the sentiments and inclinations of the great to the small, as happens to impressions made in the air or water.

Not everything was in their favour, however: on 16 January 1756 he wrote that while the inhabitants were shrewd and industrious they were somewhat barbarous because they 'lacked all other notions, despise good letters and live full of pride and vanity without any taste and flavour for study, buried deeply in ignorance'. Yet on 11 May 1759 Caracciolo commended their ability to keep their promises, and was also much struck by the military organisation of the state and the fact that most of the sons of the nobility took up

the profession of arms or entered the Academy or the body of Pages ... And all the remaining youths went to the university ... it was severely prohibited to the monastic orders to teach or open schools and the Jesuits in Piedmont representing nothing more than the Carthusians in Naples ... a great sign of a well-ordered state with wise regulations.

On the ecclesiastical front, he was full of praise for the way that the House of Savoy kept the church firmly under control. His letters to Tanucci, such as that of 25 January 1760, detail how

King Vittorio [the then ruler's father] restructured the laws, the police, people's fortunes, and finally the whole internal constitution of the country to his own liking: in ecclesiastical matters he left a simple outwardly apparent veil of priests, but in substance he kept both freedom of action and authority.

The positions of the nobility and the church were important matters for reform in the government of the Kingdom of the Two Sicilies. King Charles and Tanucci had achieved a great deal to curb both their privileges, but they were still forces to be reckoned with in Naples, and particularly so in Sicily, which operated under separate constitutional, parliamentary, legal and administrative systems. These were aspects of government that interested both Caracciolo and his minister. Caracciolo had even sent Rousseau's *Emile* to Tanucci, as can be learnt from the minister's letter of 24 July 1762, as well as letters full of professions of peace, egalitarianism and rationalism in general. This constant nagging at Tanucci to take on policies that Caracciolo thought could work in Naples was bound to get on the minister's nerves.

Neither Sardinia nor Naples was involved in the Seven Years' War. Tanucci was determined not to be dragged into it, but was extremely suspicious of the House of Savoy's well-known ambitions. Since the two countries were at peace, Caracciolo did not have much to do as a diplomat during his time in Turin: his principal brief was to keep an eye on Turin's ambitions and make sure that its rulers did not become too adventurous. As early as 1740, the Président de Brosses was writing of King Charles Emmanuel:

> He is not really strong enough to invade much at a time, but he expands little by little. His father King Victor used to say that Italy was an artichoke which had to be eaten leaf by leaf. His son will follow this maxim as much as he can, and will ally himself successively, regardless of the past, with all the great princes who will ameliorate his condition, always preferring the House of Austria to the Spaniards or ourselves, though he can only enlarge himself at Austria's expense, since the Duchy of Milan is the real objective of his greed.[8]

Tanucci was particularly concerned with two territories on which he was convinced, with good reason, that King Charles Emmanuel had designs: Piacenza and Corsica.

The city of Piacenza was a leftover from the Treaty of Aix-la-Chapelle: all contenders had set their eyes on it, small though it was in 1759, when it became clear that Ferdinand was dying. All the issues that had in fact been the secret themes of Caracciolo's first unsuccessful diplomatic venture surfaced and created a difficult political incident.

Under the terms of the treaty, Parma went to Don Philip, Charles's younger brother, who in the meantime had married Louise Elizabeth, the daughter of Louis XV, and who thought that Parma was not enough for him. He did not receive the Kingdom of the Two Sicilies, which went to Charles's second son, Ferdinand (his first son being declared an imbecile). The Empress Maria Theresa, however, very much wanted Parma; Charles Emmanuel of Savoy/Sardinia very much wanted Piacenza. When Charles succeeded Ferdinand as King of Spain, Louis XV of France had guaranteed Charles Emmanuel's claim, but this would have impinged on his son-in-law's territory, and Charles himself had no intention of allowing his younger brother Don Philip to become the King of the Two Sicilies. As Caracciolo wrote to Tanucci from Turin:

> It seems to me useless to recommend me to cultivate peaceful sentiments at this Court; it has been a sheer waste of effort. These gentlemen have ambition rooted in their bones, and they will not rest until they find an opportunity to improve their own interests.[9]

As it was, Charles massed his army along his frontiers, Louis XV worked for a compromise and Charles Emmanuel settled for money for the moment. Turin never lost interest in Piacenza and

Tanucci was very much in contact with his minister on the matter, keeping up a flood of instructions to Caracciolo, which dragged on without the issue being formally resolved right up to the last moment of Caracciolo's time there.

The question of Corsica had even wider strategic implications. The island had for some time been in revolt against its Genoese rulers, who were convinced that the government of Naples had been encouraging this, apparently with some reason: Charles had promised that he would not give the rebels support, but after the assassination of their commander, François Gaffori, in 1755, the rebels sent for the son of their exiled leader Pasquale Paoli, who happened to be an officer in the Neapolitan army. Paoli, of course, subsequently became the Garibaldi of Corsica, a romantic history that does not concern us here;[10] what does concern us is that Tanucci was worried that Charles Emmanuel had plans to seize the island of Corsica. He warned Caracciolo, and the pair were in constant touch, but the ambassador did not seem to share his chief's concerns: '[I]t does not seem probable that this Court is thinking of Corsica, because it has not yet taken the first step to establish a foothold on the coast and open up trade with the country, which is the main object.'[11] Caracciolo, however, did keep his eye on the situation, and was writing to his superior on the subject even after leaving Turin.

Tanucci's general policies were peace abroad and the continuation of reforms at home. Early on in the Seven Years' War, when William Pitt was considering the formation of an Italian League to push the Austrians out of Italy, Tanucci would not consider cooperating with Sardinia. In this, Caracciolo in Turin did not agree:

> This situation of Italian affairs is not happy, but is aggravated
> by the circumstances that the King of Naples and the King of
> Sardinia, who have greater strength than all the others, if

united in some manner could oppose the designs of their neighbours and defend themselves against the disturbers of the peace, but they happen to be distant and separated by so much territory and perhaps their respective systems are too dissimilar.[12]

Tanucci had no intention of getting involved, with the result perhaps that Caracciolo did not have very much to do. As the war progressed it became apparent that the Sardinian ambassadors in London and Paris had been particularly active diplomatically in bringing the two contending countries together, causing Tanucci to write to Losada in Madrid on 15 June 1762: 'Caracciolo is angry with the airs that the Turinese are giving themselves for having reconciled France with England.'[13] He told the king of Spain the same thing. But Caracciolo's general flow of letters was for peace and rationalism, justice and equity, and eventually provoked a belligerent reply from Tanucci on 7 August:

> War during this century has brought Spain and India to the Bourbons, has deprived the Stuarts of Great Britain, doubled the states of Piedmont and Brandenburg, placed a Sovereign in the Two Sicilies, transferred the masculine states of Austria to a female, driven the French out of true America, because Lousiana is the equivalent of the Island of Barter. And Your Excellency believes that modern wars are useless.[14]

Despite a seventeen-year age difference and their often almost polemical differences, Tanucci had gained a certain regard for Caracciolo during the long exchanges of ideas that had taken place in their diplomatic correspondence. In the general diplomatic state of change after the Treaty of Paris in 1763, it was decided to send him to the sensitive and important post of ambassador to London. In his usual blunt Tuscan way, Tanucci wrote to Losada: 'Caracciolo decides too much. I shall advise him he is for London. He has no other faults.'

The move to London was extremely leisurely. On 26 March 1763 Tanucci wrote:

> Your Excellency need not be in haste to go to London. I shall not put you to it. Stay there [Turin] until the outcome of the Piacenza dispute has been settled. You can put 4 months home leave between Turin and London.[15]

On 16 April he wrote to say that the house Caracciolo was to live in had a long lease with some years to go. But Caracciolo was always to take an immense amount of time to move from post to post. About the time Tanucci was writing to Caracciolo saying that there was no hurry, he was also writing to Catanti: 'Caracciolo is spitting on his new destiny, wailing, complaining of debts, saying he has difficulties and making demands. Oh when will these torments finish for me? He wants to come to Naples first.'[16] On 9 April Tanucci wrote to Caracciolo:

> What I know and perhaps you do not is that the post of London was very much desired and sought after; and you, without any pleading on your part, were chosen. It would seem to me that such approval of the sovereign should be a stimulus to you and a most efficacious support in countering all indecision or fantasy.[17]

Caracciolo continued dithering, but despite telling his friend Calabritto that he was not going

> to London so willingly as you imagine, it being a serious matter to me to distance myself from the beautiful skies of

Italy to go to live in a damp, dark, unhealthy climate for God knows how many years.[18]

He did eventually manage to get to London via Paris early in 1764, though he did not take his four months of home leave.

3

London

⚜

When Caracciolo did finally land in damp, dull England he was to be met by an entirely new and somewhat baffling society, as one soon learns from his early letters. Just after his arrival he wrote to his friend and Neapolitan diplomat Galiani at the Paris Embassy:

> There has been good weather and for a fortnight now the sun has gained its health and is showing here, as elsewhere, its rays with its usual pomp. The city is generally deserted, as everybody has moved to the country, so that, in the midst of eight hundred thousand souls, we are alone, reduced each of us to staying at home or obliged to play a barbarous game of cards at the Imperial Ambassador's or the Dutch Minister's. Here is this great society that you were praising! Can you not understand that the English are by nature not sociable? An English person goes to meet another English person, be it a gentleman or a lady, to take a walk, to dance, to sing, to play at cards, to make love, to do business, but never to talk. This pleasure or need does not enter into the heads of the British; your lovely witty stories would be lost in London.[1]

The correspondence between Galiani and Caracciolo was always somewhat exaggerated, for reasons dictated by the needs of wit, but there was no doubt that the new ambassador found himself in a whole new world. What struck him most was the wholehearted dedication of the English to the imperative demands of commerce. As he wrote to Tanucci, 'In substance the British Government is a democratic republic whose God is Commerce and France is the Devil,'[2] or, as he put it more pithily to Galiani, 'In London they sell stones by the pound.'[3] This was a dedication to business alien to the spirit that reigned in Naples and far in excess of the mercantalist efficiency that Caracciolo had met with in Turin, but it was to make a deep impression on him during his mission in London, a mission closely concerned with matters of trade and commerce. It is also worth pointing out that, although Caracciolo was not alone in noting Britain's overwhelming preoccupation with commercial questions, at the time the distinction between 'economics' and 'philosophy' was still blurred and very much within the sphere of a would-be Enlightened interest.

Such dedication to money without further ado was novel to the ambassador, with the result that English society appeared cold at first. As he wrote to Galiani:

> Despite their philosophy which does them honour, as a nation they are basically Teutonic, and thus need to be hammered on the head to be made to see reason ... So that they are by nature hostile to hospitality, and extremely hostile to foreigners.[4]

He did, however, get out into society. In that same letter to Galiani, he continued:

> I went to the horse races at Newmarket. There I enjoyed myself reflecting on the vagaries of men and in particular on the national character of the English in reducing these things into a system to the level of folly and passion and taking them

seriously. I have seen the greatest gentlemen dressed as grooms, deeming themselves honoured to resemble one of that class, all mixed together with others of every sort of rank and condition, discuss, dispute and consult gravely among themselves whether one may give a certain horse three or four pounds weight of advantage. What do you think? That I am a goose? ... I shall write you a separate chapter about women on another occasion.

He invited Galiani to visit him a short while afterwards, though the visit did not take place until a later date:

Come! You will not need to spend a farthing. Come to my house. You will lack nothing ... plays, operas, balls, Parliament, and the new greenery in the countryside. Write and come! I shall make you laugh and enjoy yourself. We shall make a tour together of the best things in the provinces: the universities, the country houses, the men of letters, the politicians, the w[hores] ... We shall mix the sacred with the profane. And make a good soup of it.[5]

The reality did not live up to the promises, however, as he wrote later:

We have a bad Opera and some subscription balls, for which one pays, and which can well give an idea of the Day of Judgement, painted in that famous picture of Michaelangelo's in the Sistine Chapel.[6]

Caracciolo also became embroiled in social chores for his friend Galiani, who sent him over from Paris various persons to sort out in England. Trying to find a military position for the ex-lover of a certain Madame de Saint-Vast, a ridiculous old woman covered in rouge, 'with two bare black boobs', was a particular bugbear, involving the minister of war, Lady Holland and Madame Geoffrin before he refused to take the matter any further. Another was a certain 'Muscovite' reputed to be indomitable in matters of love, but after a certain flutter of interest this gentleman disappeared from the scene.

As time went on, Caracciolo came to terms with the new ambience. Casanova noted approvingly in the *History of His Life* that Caracciolo, together with lords Baltimore and Pembroke, was wise enough to refuse payment to some entrancing, though penniless, young ladies that Casanova had come to know because they had been refused favours in advance.[7]

He also had some work to do.

As far as the Neapolitan government was concerned, Caracciolo's main task in London was to negotiate a commercial treaty with the government of Great Britain – a difficult job at the best of times, which these were not. Two other areas of work required his attention. During his first year in London there was a serious shortage of grain in the Kingdom of the Two Sicilies due to a disastrous harvest and worse administration. This involved him in negotiating for, buying up, transporting and arguing about large quantities of grain to help solve this short-term crisis. He was also deeply involved in trying to develop the Sicilian silk trade in the English market, an extension of the work he had started in his years in Turin.

The story of the projected commercial treaty is long and intricate. Even though the importance of southern Mediterranean trade was diminishing for Britain, it was still important and, *vis à vis* the Two Sicilies, very much balanced in favour of the British. The first attempt at an assessment of this bias was made by Sir William Hamilton, the British ambassador in Naples, in answer to Lord Halifax's request of May 1765. The following year it was estimated that the balance in Britain's favour was to the enormous sum of £416,268 (though this did include money for the grain that was being imported from England by Caracciolo to cover the grain dearth in this period).[8] This imbalance of trade, a commercial evil in the age of mercantalism, together with the ever-present problems of contraband and the closely connected question of rights to inspect ships of other nations, were major problems for the Neapolitan side in any trade negotiations, though far less so for the British. Treaties of commerce had always come to grief against juridical, customary and treaty restrictions concerning inspection of ships of other countries, which resulted in the flourishing of contraband without any effective control: this occasioned great loss to the national treasuries of smaller nations, as it was known that the fleets of France and England did well by the practice. And the same applied to the corsairs. As Smollet has it:

> That the Barbary States are advantageous to the marine power is certain. If they were suppressed the little states of Italy etc would have much more of the carrying trade ... for it is for our share of advantage that we cultivate the piratical states of Barbary, and mainly purchase transports of them, thus acknowledging them masters of the Mediterranean.[9]

The major obstacle to any change was that Britain did not want them. All discussion was referred back to the Treaty of Madrid of 1667, when Spain had granted Britain the status of most favoured nation. Naples at the time was a province of Spain, and any inspections of British (or incidentally French) ships by Spanish or Neapolitan ones were prohibited. The British also demanded the reintroduction of the *giudice delegato* (a specifically delegated judge, abolished in 1759) in commercial cases that involved British interests instead of the newly instituted *Supremo Magistrato di Commercio*, which was considered inefficient and open to bribery.

Such was the background to Caracciolo's brief from Tanucci, who thought that British imports from the Sicilies should have been interesting enough to carry the negotiations. In reality the British were not at all interested and Caracciolo pushed ahead with the negotiations with a certain haste, which, complicated by the fact that he had forgotten his secret code books, leaving them behind in Turin, and could not read certain restraining advice that came to him in code from his more experienced chief, meant that the first stage in the negotiations were in a bad state by August of 1764.

Preparations for the negotiations started early. By mid-March Tanucci's correspondence was already taken up with the question of the possible treaty; in fact, he sent Caracciolo a memorandum on the subject, even suggesting that he made discreet use with Lord Halifax of the affair of certain British ships that had been protecting Tunisian pirates at Livorno under the command of one Commodore Harrison, which had created a diplomatic incident later on at Malta.[10] A month later (24 April 1764) he was writing of equal treatment of inspections for Neapolitan ships in London and British ships in Sicilian ports (on a technical point of whether they had reached their final port of call or not) and on the non-applicability of Spanish treaties to Neapolitan ships. By 5 May Tanucci's instructions, despite the fact that they were not in code, were becoming much more specific and are worth quoting in more detail:

> Your Excellency, as I wrote to you the other time, can open discussions on a Commercial Treaty. These gentlemen should tell us what they want from us and we what we wish to give them. They are more practical and experienced than us, who will always be passive ... [The French and the English destroy us with their customs dues] ... We must maintain our position as much as we can; but when they concede

inspections without distinction, I see that we shall have to do something for them, particularly if they agree to take from us an amount of silk, pitch, wool, manna [a substance made from the sap of the ash tree], raisins, liquorice equivalent to the amount of goods they take from us ... We are virgins as far as treaties are concerned and are free, and we have no superior power [i.e. Spain].

On 2 June 1764 Tanucci explained that when he had talked about ship inspections he had thought that Caracciolo had read his coded memorandum: he explained that the English had no *privilege* of non-inspection in any treaty. However, Caracciolo, he wrote, should continue with the negotiation for the commercial treaty: if this did not work they would try to make themselves self-sufficient. His next letter, of 9 June 1764, announced the shipment of two new codebooks, one via Germany and one via Spain, which would allow Caracciolo to read the famous memorandum that he could not read before. The letter went on to give him advice on how to draft the document he was to write for Lord Halifax. It is curious, given Caracciolo's character, that towards the end of the letter Tanucci felt he needed to write: 'I see (and I am sincere in this) in your Excellency a fear and a perplexity that compromises the efficacy of any negotiation you undertake.'

What Tanucci was unaware of was that Caracciolo, on his own initiative and not having read the coded memorandum, had sent a memorial, dated 14 June 1764, of his own to Lord Halifax in French that did not respect the spirit of his minister's brief and was not couched in terms designed to attract Halifax.[11] It was a plain and forthright letter between two reasonable beings for the establishment of a commercial treaty, recognising that the Two Sicilies exported to Britain raw materials and imported manufactured goods from Britain with the balance very much in the latter's favour, but that the trade and the profit was greatly damaged by contraband, which could be avoided if the British accepted inspections of their ships in Neapolitan ports, which Naples had been asking for in the context of a general commercial treaty. Apart from Caracciolo not having read Tanucci's coded memorandum, a contributing factor was probably parallel anti-contraband pressure building up in France. In effect, Caracciolo had already broached the subject of inspections with Halifax as early as February, and had left a memorial with him that had not received an answer (and was therefore considered rejected); he probably resuscitated the idea when he heard that his counterpart in Paris was negotiating the same subject with the French government. Whatever the details, Halifax considered that Caracciolo's latest memorial confused the question of inspections (which he considered already rejected) with a Commercial Treaty and called off the negotiation, and Tanucci reprimanded Caracciolo for exceeding his brief and being 'un-diplomatic'.

Criticisms began to be expressed in July. Tanucci wrote to the now King Charles III of Spain:

> The Regency did not like part of the memorial that Caracciolo presented to milord Halifax for the discussion of the Commercial Treaty. Your Majesty with your customary wisdom had ordained that this treaty could not to any great extent involve ship inspections, that only and expressly that government did not desire: those were the orders given to Caracciolo; but he talked of contraband so openly that he revealed the objective of ship inspection though he did not mention it by name; realising that he had gone too far, he tried to excuse himself by claiming that the world was by now too illuminated, that Halifax had already suspected our intention, that sincerity was the best choice and that today it was necessary to deceive with the truth.[12]

But in his next letter to Caracciolo (21 July 1764), Tanucci was sticking to his guns: he had received three copies of the memorial sent to Halifax and hoped there would soon be a reply. It was more than a month later that the criticisms began to be expressed directly to Caracciolo. On 28 July 1764 he wrote that some in Naples would have preferred less 'sincerity' when dealing with the question of contraband; he also said that he was working on an answer to Halifax's eventual reply and had some strong remarks about the arrogance of Lord Sandwich. By 7 August 1764 Halifax had formally rejected Caracciolo's memorial and Tanucci was informing the king that he would do what he could to put the pieces together again. His letter to Caracciolo on 11 August 1764 was far more explicit. It was an I-told-you-so letter. 'Mylord's reply shows that you should not have spoken so clearly. But your Excellency had it in your head to talk clearly and without mystery.' Tanucci told Caracciolo he must forget about ship inspections and get back to inventing another negotiation for a commercial treaty of reciprocal advantage without useless empty threats. This was a sound rebuke, which was repeated on 21 August 1764, Tanucci citing his previous correspondence in evidence that he had never briefed Caracciolo to give emphasis to ship inspections or contraband in the negotiations; however, the negotiations had to be continued and he would come back on how best to do this in his next letter. On the same day, however, Tanucci was writing to the Spanish king that Caracciolo was still contemplating answering Halifax in what he considered an unsatisfactory way, but that he, Tanucci, had decided to intervene with a memorandum designed to keep the communications on the right track. On 4 September 1764 Caracciolo received a new brief from Tanucci (a copy was sent to the King of Spain on the same date): enough, he wrote, had been said about inspections and the Treaty of Madrid; what was needed was a new treaty such as the ones that the new Kingdom of the Two Sicilies had with

Sweden and the Ottoman Empire, a treaty that gave tangible commercial advantage to the two nations.

And that, in effect, was that. The negotiations were not abandoned, but never came to anything. The balance of trade remained with the British, but as the importance of the Mediterranean was declining a commercial treaty with Naples was not a burning issue with London: real commercial interest was now concentrated in the American Colonies and the West and East Indies. Though Tanucci became involved personally with the negotiations, he did not have the clout to achieve anything. Caracciolo suggested that he threaten to cut off imports of English salted codfish as a pawn in the negotiations and the suggestion was even put to the King of Spain, but that was hardly likely to daunt Halifax. Sporadic talks were held over the years on commercial issues, including the reintroduction of the *giudice delegato*, but contraband was always a stumbling block (despite the official reprimand that Caracciolo had received for giving emphasis to it in his negotiations), as Sir William Hamilton wrote on 7 June 1766:

> The Court of Naples is extremely desirous to make a new Treaty of Commerce with Us, and promises Us any Advantages in it, provided We will permit Them to visit our very small ships ... Their chief Motive for this is, that They have the same power over the ships of France [French and British ships had equal status in the Treaty of Madrid], who traffic greatly in contraband and insists on being treated as the most favoured nation.[13]

There is an interesting letter describing these contraband and illegal activities written by Caracciolo at a later date (11 March 1784) when he was Viceroy of Sicily.[14] It concerned a certain Captain Scarnicchia, who raised a false English flag in Palermo harbour, took on board a wanted murderer for the price of

20 ounces (and showed him to all comers), and escaped to Trapani to take on a cargo of salt before Caracciolo, who was powerless unless he came ashore, could organise anything. Eventually, Scarnicchia had to leave hurriedly, only half laden, without paying and without quarantine clearance: Caracciolo, without much optimism, asked Naples to protest formally to His Britannic Majesty. At the same time, Caracciolo was willing to make representations at Court to concede one of the British requirements, the reintroduction of the *guidice delegato*. But there was no political will for the treaty on the English side (their interest was in the West and East Indies) and the talks dragged on till 1790, when they were finally broken off.

Meanwhile, still in the commercial sector, Caracciolo had been playing merchant, financier and shipper in the corn market since the moment he had set foot in England. Not only had the harvest of 1763 in the Two Sicilies failed badly, but, according to Tanucci, the inefficiency, the bad faith and the sheer greed of the organisations in charge of distributing corn to the populace had created serious riot conditions both in Sicily and on the mainland. It was a real emergency. By 14 February 1764 Tanucci was already answering Caracciolo's letter of 20 January of that year ('I cannot express the consolation that came to me on receiving your revered letter of the 20th ult'[15]) and went on to curse the criminal negligence of the administrators, hoping that Caracciolo would be able to persuade a 'generous Nation that takes pleasure in syllogisms and humanity' to help out in this good cause. On the day this letter was sent, Caracciolo had already ordered 200,000 *tumoli* of corn, and Tanucci rushed his next letter (21 February 1764) to assure his ambassador that he had only just received the post after a full month and, as a result, the money he had sent would not cover the 200,000 *tumuli* and another order for corn that also had to be paid, but that he was enclosing all his official orders so that Caracciolo would be able to show them to the traders in London as assurance that payment would be forthcoming and prompt. In March, Tanucci was asking for even more corn, but in April Caracciolo confirmed the last shipment. The crisis was over and Tanucci appeared to agree with Caracciolo's comments about agriculture in the Two Sicilies being 'neglected and even poorly helped by government and the laws', going on to express views with which his ambassador would certainly have agreed when he wrote: 'The truth is that in the Kingdom, as throughout Italy and Spain, there are not enough people who cultivate. The Church is the mother of inertia.'[16]

The crisis may have been over, but the situation was turning sour. At the beginning of May Tanucci told Caracciolo that his corn had arrived late and that there had been a great deal of sharp dealing among the international dealers, on which Tanucci had been quick to stamp. Then there were complaints that too much corn had been imported, and here as well Tanucci stepped in to calm the waters. There had been a great deal of administrative chaos, but again Tanucci made it his personal duty to make sure the invoices were paid. But the real problem began with the summer when an epidemic broke out. Towards the end of July, Tanucci wrote to London to say that the kingdom had been afflicted with a terrible epidemic, which had caused the death of some 5,000 people. Suspicion fell on imported corn. The English corn, which had arrived late, was still on board ship and 'more than 60,000 *tumuli* sent by your Excellency' was condemned to be thrown into the sea:

> You can see the fight these gouty-handed officials put up when they are forced to pay. They have already asked me if Your Excellency affirms that he embarked the corn in good condition. I replied that you did. They also asked if Your Excellency had had the corn inspected by expert appraisers. I said I did not know.

Tanucci went on to assure Caracciolo that the court would guarantee payment.[17] A week later, the minister was at pains to reassure Caracciolo that he was not at fault, and that he had been 'the most prudent, the most exact of all those who had been involved in providing us with grain'. The fact remains that many invoices were not paid for some time and Caracciolo felt uncomfortable, though not guilty. He had written to Galiani in Paris (5 August 1764):

> In this country a commercial question is a national question. It is true that corn, in the heat of that climate can suffer; but why did they ask for it and order it in the month of March? And then they kept it on board without unloading it; in the port where there was not a breath of air they left a ship for five weeks; and then they complain they found it smelled.[18]

Caracciolo was right about the British commercial mind: the argument dragged on for seven years, but Naples was forced to pay every penny in the end.

It was during this major grain crisis that the malfunctioning of the agricultural system in the Two Sicilies became particularly evident, showing up the privileges, delays and the corruption that plagued the administration and resulted in evident injustice. The social tension that was the consequence had an immediate effect on Tanucci's policies (leading him to seek an increased royal power as the only effective way to cut through the corrupt, inefficient, privileged, bureaucratic institutions as he tried to reform the situation in the kingdom), and the intellectuals, Genovesi in the lead, were beginning to argue that free trade was the key to dissolving the feudal control of agriculture. Both these lines of thought would be close to Caracciolo's own way of thinking in the future.

In between major policy issues, Caracciolo was concerned with apparently less weighty concerns, though they were doubtless part and parcel of the diplomatic work of the time. He bought, secretly and free of taxes, six horses for Queen Charlotte of England in the Kingdom of the Two Sicilies (this had been the subject of some correspondence with Tanucci). He recommended suitable local Neapolitan businessmen to act as consuls in London and Tanucci passed their names on to the king of Spain for final approval. He also certified the legitimacy of the marquisate of the lover of the sister of one of Casanova's mistresses, whom this latter had extricated from gaol for debt,[19] and gave character references to Halifax and Hamilton and sent the normal political gossip from England back to his chief in Italy. His next major activity, however, was concerned with the silk trade.

Caracciolo's two memoranda on the subject were really two long letters setting out practical recommendations for the improvement of the silk industry in Sicily on the basis of some international market research.[20] Briefly, Caracciolo the diplomat and philosopher was advocating the introduction of a new small-wheel technique into the production cycle that would render the presentation of Sicilian silk much more acceptable to English trade and therefore greatly increase exports to Britain. The memoranda may have been occasioned by a request from the regency government in Naples, who were interested in the development of the Sicilian silk trade and had been experiencing difficulties with the controlling authorities on the island: it is possible that they had asked Caracciolo for a report from the hub of international commercial activity that was London and passed it on to Fogliani, who was then viceroy in Sicily. It is also possible that the initiative was Caracciolo's own, in an attempt to gain some kudos after the abject failure of the negotiations with Halifax. He was on good mercantalist ground by choosing the Sicilian silk for improvement – this was a solid traditional industry, but had seen better days, and he had already made a start when he was in Turin. However, it is also possible that the move came from Neapolitan and Sicilian merchants resident in London, who would have been interested in the market, aware of the administrative problems in Sicily, of the technical problems that existed and in close contact with Caracciolo. Or it may have been a combination of causes.

The fact is, Caracciolo made a series of visits to the silk warehouses in the city with experts and saw samples from various localities. Southern silk was excellent in quality, but not produced in the right form for the English textile industry. This was due to not having the right equipment, which it was the government's duty to provide. The Piedmontese had the right expensive equipment for organzines, which commanded the highest prices, but the Sicilian industry was not ready for this yet. Caracciolo proposed at least to adopt the size of skein that the English market preferred and was prepared to pay more for, rather than the larger one the Sicilians made, which the English workers 'hated'. There was no problem in this: the government simply had to burn all the old wheels and then remake small wheels at public expense. He also recommended exporting directly to London rather than indirectly through Livorno, where middlemen were doing illicit things. His memoranda were transmitted in June 1764 to the *Supremo Magistratura* in Naples and thence to the *Consolati della Seta*, where they stirred up a hornet's nest among the vested interests. Everything was invented against the recommendations: Sicilian silk was made from black mulberries, not white like Piedmontese silk; small wheels had been tried before on other occasions and had not worked. They were rejected in February next year. Other vested interests were concerned with the costs involved, the laws and customs, and the fact that France had most of The Sicilies' trade, much of it through Genoa. Nothing was done. Vested interests and conservatism were awaiting Caracciolo in Sicily. Bengalese silk was about to cancel Sicilian silk manufacturing.

Caracciolo's contact with the silk industry in London brought him face to face with 'democracy' in action. He was struck by what he saw of the strike of the silk workers in 1765, fomented by Pitt and brought on by the Duke of Bedford's convincing the Lords to refuse a ban on French textile imports, which had been demanded by the workers. As he wrote to Galiani in July 1765:

> I forgot to tell you that there being afoot a revendication of the silk workers who demanded the total prohibition of French textile imports and twelve thousand of whom had therefore gathered outside the doors of the House of Commons, the Duke of Bedford opposed the act and had it rejected after it had been approved by the Commons. Whereupon they broke his head with a good stoning and then stormed off to burn his palace, where the soldiery needed to use great energy to save him and his house from the fury of those people since they could not fire at them. The law prohibits this until the rioters have been read a law of George I's: until this has been done, there is the death penalty for firing for officers and men. In the meantime the Duke of Bedford was in evident danger of being lynched from a column of his own palace. What does it matter! These are small incidents that are born of liberty. The people were the enemy of the Duke of Bedford *et non est hostis publicus* ['and not a public enemy']; so magistrates had to be approached rather than reaction taken against events. It would seem to me that God, having banished liberty in all monarchical governments, has left it to console us just in Poland and England.[21]

In the autumn of 1767 he took a holiday. A brief glimpse of it comes to light in Casanova's memoirs and is quoted here in full.[22]

> The person I was delighted to see in Spa was the Marchese Caraccioli [*sic*], whom I had left in London. He had obtained

a leave of absence from his Court, and he was amusing himself in Spa. He was a man of sound intelligence, kind, humane, compassionate, a friend to youth – male or female, he did not care – but not in excess. He did not gamble, but he liked gamesters who knew how to play, and he despised dupes. Being of this happy character, he made the Marquis d'Aragon's fortune. He vouched for his name and his nobility to a fifty-year old English widow who was then in Spa and who fell in love with him. On the word of the Ambassador Caraccioli, she married him and brought him sixty thousand pounds sterling as her dowry. She can only have fallen in love with his six feet of stature and with the proud name of d'Aragon, for he had neither wit nor manners and his legs were covered with venereal sores; but since he always wore boots the Englishwoman cannot have seen them until after their wedding. I saw him some time afterward in Marseilles, and some years later he went to Modena, where he bought two fiefs. His wife died and left him rich. I believe he is still alive. The excellent Caraccioli congratulated himself on having thus made the fortune of an adventurer, whose name was Dragon. By borrowing an *A*, he had made himself d'Aragon.

A month or so later Casanova was in Paris in bad financial trouble and in receipt of *letters de cachet* from Louis XVI meaning that he had to leave France forthwith: he elected to go to Madrid, and Caracciolo supplied him with introductory letters to the Prince della Cattolica, the Duke of Losada and the Marquis of Mora Pignatelli.[23]

His enquiring mind was in communication with many like Abbé Galiani and attracted Italian intellectuals, writers and scientists who were either resident or passing through London. Most of these sought or received help from the ambassador.

Pietro and Paolo Verri, for example, who travelled to Paris and London in 1766 and 1767, were taken under Caracciolo's wing:

> I go sometimes to Marquis Caracciolo's, the Naples Ambassador, a man who had lava in his veins like all of his nation, and beyond that a man of real merit and heart, as far as I can judge in a few visits. Frisi has written hundreds of things about me and his friendship has dictated such praises that it has placed me in the uncomfortable position of being a man of letters and, what is more, a man of wit. He has written that I am profound in the most erudite jurisprudence, that I enjoy high estimation in my country [he was from Milan], that I have had printed books that have been well received and that I have a very interesting book currently in the process of being printed. After all that it seems that I am presenting myself to a cannon-royal in the person of my lord Marquis Caracciolo. He is very much alive, although old, and always wants to talk Himself and, if I am not too malign, not very eager to let a young man shine whose head he suspects too full of ideas. I have been to lunch with him; I have paid him some visits, but it does not seem that he warms to me as much as Frisio promised.[24]

One has the feeling that the Marquis might have been somehow right. Anyhow, Paolo Frisi was another matter. He was an intellectual of European standing arriving at physics and particularly hydrophysics from ethics, metaphysics and mathematics. He had been elected a member of the Royal Society in 1757, but it was in 1766, when in London on an extended stay, that he met Caracciolo and they began a long correspondence[25] that covered subjects as diverse as mathematics, astronomy and the controversy between Hume and Rousseau. Caracciolo introduced him to new members of the Royal Society, presented his work *De gravitate universali corporum* to Morton (who was then president) and also shared his friendship with Franklin, Maty, D'Alembert (Frisi was already in correspondence with him) and La Grange, who was passing through the capital (Caracciolo was later to try to persuade La Grange to teach mathematics in Palermo). Other Italian intellectuals were part of the circle, such as Lomellini and Mazzei, but very little material survives, and Michele Torcia, later a social commentator and reformer, was the embassy secretary at the time. Almost all Caracciolo's private correspondence has gone missing and the official letters rarely mention cultural life. Just occasionally one gets a small glimpse when, for instance, Caracciolo was publicly shamed by an exhibition of ignorance before the Royal Society by the Marchese di Santo Lucido. He wrote to Galiani on 2 February 1765:

> Santo Lucido has here sent to the Royal Society a dissertation in perfidious Latin on the ebb and flow of the sea, the silliest and most puerile thing to have come out since the abuse of the press. Nobody has replied to it here: what annoys me only is that they think that the author belongs to our intellectual class, from which they deduce the miserable state of the sciences in Italy.[26]

Such was his shame that even Tanucci felt he ought to commiserate: 'I am sorry for the ridicule that the Marchese di S. Lucido has caused there with his book.'[27] Some of the ambassador's contact with literary life savoured of the dramatic – to be expected if you counted the tragedian Count Vittorio Alfieri among your friends. While in London and not wildly riding horses, Alfieri was very publicly flaunting an affair with Penelope Pitt, the wife of Lord Ligonier. While showing off during a ride one Saturday morning with Caracciolo, Alfieri dislocated his shoulder and broke his collar-bone; by Tuesday, still in much pain, he was called to the door of Prince Masserano's box at the Italian theatre by the appearance of Lord Ligonier and disappeared with him to Green Park, where a duel was fought and the injured husband obtained satisfaction. After returning to the theatre for a short period, he left to regain the arms of his lover, who had been repudiated by her husband; he remained with her for some considerable time before, at a very late hour, seeking out Caracciolo and the Sardinian ambassador (Alfieri was Piedmontese). Caracciolo was eventually found at home, roused, and forced to spend the rest of the night dispensing advice on what Alfieri should do. On the Wednesday morning, despite negative advice from Prince Masserano, the Sardinian ambassador and Caracciolo, Alfieri determined to marry Lady Ligonier. But a problem arose: she would not, though she loved him to distraction, because if she did there would be a dreadful scandal – she had been having an affair with a jockey in the Ligonier household for three years, who, when he had been discarded, had spied on them and was the cause of their discovery. So the affair came to an end and Alfieri left the country.[28]

Many years later, when writing his autobiography, Alfieri described Caracciolo as 'more than a father in affairs of love during my second stay in London of more than seven months, during which time I found myself in extraordinary and embarrassing circumstances.'[29] There was, it is true, a 35-year age gap between the two, but apparently such a bond was established that they were even to exchange coded letters in Florentine periodicals of the early 1780s.[30]

On 5 May 1769 Caracciolo received a despatch from Tanucci appointing him ambassador extraordinary in Paris. After nearly six years of interesting, but not exactly successful, life in England he was appointed at the age of 56 to what he must have considered his final posting. As always, he did not leave immediately: in this case he had to wait until the arrival of his replacement, Prince

Pignatelli, which did not happen for well over a year. On 15 August 1771, a few days before leaving, he wrote a long last letter to Galiani describing the arrangements for his departure. Among other things he wrote of the enthusiasm for Naples and the Neapolitans of Sir William Hamilton and his first wife (not the famous Emma) who were on brief home leave, but the letter is particularly interesting for its description of the return of Captain Cook with Sir Joseph Banks after their three-year voyage to the South Seas to study astronomy, botany and natural history. The letter gives a brief summary of the voyage and says that he had seen and talked to the protagonists often in London.[31] Six days later, on 21 August, Caracciolo left London with eight magnificent horses to take possession of the elegant apartment that had been prepared for him in the Hotel Broglio, in the country he was to consider his spiritual homeland.

4

Paris

✣

From the records it would not seem that Caracciolo's abundant energy was overtaxed with intricate diplomatic issues or complex official problems during his nine years in Paris, but his distinguished involvement in the literary, philosophical, scientific, anti-clerical and economic activities of the leading *salons* of Paris did much for the reputation of the Kingdom of the Two Sicilies, and indeed he and the Abbé Galiani were the kingdom's most famous exports.

Caracciolo was at home in the *salons* of Madame Geoffrin, Baron d'Holbach, Helvétius, Mademoiselle Lespinasse and Madame d'Epinay,[1] to name but the most prominent, but he was friends with all the *philosophes*, though closest probably to D'Alembert, and their memoirs and letters are full of his name and Galiani's. It is worth quoting some of these because they illustrate the extent to which he had become one of them and go some way to explain his later frustration when faced with almost unimaginably different situations when viceroy in Sicily. Madame Necker, for instance, had this to say of Caracciolo:

His conversation always connected with other people's; abbé Galiani's was only concerned with extraordinary things: Caracciolo always saw common things from a new point of view.[2]

The French politician, Duc de Lévis, also admired him:

> No one was more animated or had more brilliant conversation than that Italian – he had the wit of four, gesticulated like eight and made the noise of twenty. He filled a whole *salon* by himself; but his gaiety was so natural that it put nobody out; he had an original way of seeing and expressing things and an inexhaustible fund of good jokes which had nothing of spite or bitterness.[3]

A fuller picture is given by Caracciolo's friend, the poet Marmontel:

> At first sight Caracciolo's physiognomy had that thick massive appearance that one uses when painting stupidity. To animate his eyes and disentangle his features, you had to make him speak. But then, as fast as that lively, penetrating, luminous intelligence with which he was endowed was aroused, one saw it breaking out in scintillating sparks; and the finesse, the gaiety, the originality of the thought, the naturalness of the expression, the grace of his smile, the feeling in his glance combined to bestow an amiable, ingenious, and interesting character to his ugliness. He spoke our language badly and with difficulty, but he was eloquent in his own; and when he could not find a French term he borrowed the word, the thought or the image he needed from Italian. Like this he very often enriched his conversation with thousands of fearless picturesque expressions which made us envious. He accompanied them also with that Neapolitan gesticulation that, with the abbé Galiani, animated their expression so well, and one said of both of them that they possessed wit right down to the end of their finger-tips. Both of them were also full of excellent stories, almost all of them of first-rate, moral and profound sense. Caracciolo had made a philosophic study

of men; but he had observed them more in politics and as statesmen rather than from the point of view of moral satire. He had seen the morals of nations, their customs and their policies on a grand scale; and if he quoted some particular traits it was only as an example and in support of the results that formed his opinion. With inexhaustible riches of knowledge and a highly amiable nature when it came to sharing them, he had to our eyes something more – the merit of being an excellent man.[4]

It was the humanity of Caracciolo that distinguished him from Galiani, who was certainly the superior wit, critic and scientist, but always a bit malign. He wrote to Madame d'Epinay, untruthfully, of Caracciolo, 'Caracciolo is always Caracciolo: useless to society, agreeable in society,'[5] but society itself had different thoughts, best expressed perhaps by Marmontel again:

> None of us would have thought of making abbé Galiani his friend; each of us would have coveted the friendship of Caracciolo, and I who have enjoyed it for a long time cannot say enough about how desirable it was.[6]

As is evident from this selection of letters and memories Caracciolo was very much at home in Paris and appreciated there. His work does not seem to have extended him much, but, though the kingdom he represented was not a major power, its ambassador was held in high repute. The view that some of his success in Paris might be put down to his being seen as something of a buffoon, as a picturesque aristocrat from the deep south of Europe (see *Il Dizionario Bibliografico degli Italiani*), does not ring true. It would hardly justify his name being chosen to underwrite the violent attack against his friend Necker contained in the fraudulent pamphlet *Lettre de M. le Marquis de Caracioli à M. d'Alembert*, actually written by the Comte de Gimoard in 1781, just after Caracciolo had left Paris for Sicily.

Much later, in 1782, the Marchese di Licciocara[7] was to publish a list of his Parisian friends in *Lo Spione italiano* as follows: Fontanelle, Montasquieu, Voltaire, Rousseau, Helvetius, Condillac, Diderot, D'Alembert, Marmontel, Mabley, Condorcet, Linguet, Turgot, Mirabeau, Necker and others; among the foreigners, Franklin, Hume, Sterne, Haller; among the Italians, Goldoni, Spallanzani, Mattei, Metastasio.

The easiest way to track Caracciolo's life in Paris is through his letters and particularly those to Galiani, who was in Naples while Caracciolo was there. Almost all of Galiani's to Caracciolo have been lost, but the latter's are constant despite distractions, laziness and even an intellectual dispute at one point, though such was his total abandon to the new life when he first arrived that it was many months before he got round to sending his first letter to his friend. He had, in fact, left London on 21 August 1771, but his first letter was dated 21 December 1771 from Fontainbleau.[8]

> As soon as I received your letter in the midst of balls, hunts, theatres, dinners, etc., I took up my pen worrying that you could have had the slightest doubt about our old friendship. My dear friend, you have certainly given me no offence of any kind, neither could you have done, because I know your good heart and your good ways. In any case, as a matter of principle I never measure my friends by a goldsmith's scales but rather a miller's steelyard.

And he plunged into his news, much of which was concerned with the end of the so-called Maupeou *coup d'état* and the struggle between Louis XV and the Parlements. It is interesting to quote in that it shows the reformer Caracciolo was always a die-hard monarchist:

The *affaire* of the Parlements is considered finished ... The son of the chancellor [the son of Maupeou], the 'quondam' president, has been made a cavalry colonel; the son of president Pellettier a captain. In short, the dead are dead. This is the result of the anglomania of these toga'd gentlemen! They have delivered so many fine speeches, said so many beautiful things, made so many excellent calculations; but they have forgotten to calculate that Louis XV had at his beck and call three hundred thousand men, and that the grace of the sovereign in this country is really to be compared to the grace of God, and when it is lacking man immediately falls into mortal sin and risks plunging into hell. Outside the Court in France there is no hope in looking for health, just as outside the Ark in the Flood.

His monarchism had nothing to do with religion, of course, and his letters to Tanucci in Naples included anticlerical as well as all sorts of other advice, as they had always done. From Paris he wrote that the principal point from which to continue the reform of the Kingdom of Naples was 'to reduce to within just limits the rabble of the monks and the tyranny of the Roman Curia and to make the ecclesiastics pay'; he went on to say that the poor must have their burden lightened and the rich be made to contribute to the exchequer, that the *catasto* (land survey) should be reformed, and that education should be removed from the control of monks.[9] While his letters to Tanucci did continue to give his latest thoughts to his minister, they were more illustrations of his developing philosophy rather than lectures on how to govern the Kingdom of the Two Sicilies, as they had been earlier. At this stage it is interesting to note Caracciolo's growing disdain of aristocrats in general and from his own country in particular and his praise for the middle classes:

by experience in all the countries I have been to I have always found the middle class, the class in the middle of society, the most capable, best behaved, most virtuous.[10]

His dislike of the priesthood culminated when the papal nuncio accepted invitations from Madame du Barry, the king's mistress, who had decided she wished to have foreign ambassadors to dine. All, for one reason or another, felt they could justify this, with the exception of the Spanish ambassador and Caracciolo; then the papal nuncio was won over by the hope of the restitution of Avignon and the possible gain of a large abbey for himself, which gave rise to a letter to Tanucci about the nuncio courting the courtesan.[11] His anticlericalism, which was general in 'Enlightened' society, brought him particularly close to D'Alembert and Helvétius, whose funeral Caracciolo describes in a letter to Galiani of 10 January 1772:

You ask for news of your friends. I can assure you you are often mentioned in the usual assemblies I attend (Holbach, Madame de Geoffrin, Madamoiselle Lespinasse, etc.); and they still remember your sayings. Helvétius died to the great sorrow of his friends and all the fellowship of good people. He died with that philosophical steadfastness and persuasion that was well known to you. His wife would in no way consent to the requests of many of his friends that a priest should be present, saying that she had promised that to her husband. The incident passed off lightly. As soon as the sick man expired they sent in haste for the parish priest, who came and [testified] the unexpected death. Nevertheless [he was told that] the sick man, since he had died intestate as a result of an unforeseen accident, had made it known that he intended to donate eight hundred francs to the poor of the parish, to be given in cash to the parish priest, and the funeral cortège was decent. So the sop was given to Cerberus. The fore-mentioned parish priest was happy and reassured all the company, except Madame Helvétius who refused to see him, with pious words, exhorting them to trust in the mercy of God. This was a serious step, because Helvétius was a person 'in evidence' and retractions would have been desired, as had happened with Montesquieu. He left a hundred thousand francs in income to be divided between his two daughters, who will each of them have a million and a half in dowry. Madame, who, despite the request of her husband, generously did not even wish the notary to come to the funeral for fear that he should be disturbed, remains badly off. She will have twenty thousand francs. The second part of the book *L'Esprit* remains in her hands, which will perhaps be printed in Holland. There also remains by Helvétius a small poem on the subject *Bonheur*, but it is incomplete. They say it contains beautiful things and that his greatest talent was in poetry.

Not all his time was concerned with literary matters, though surviving references in non-official correspondence and diaries strongly suggest so. There was an official aspect to his life, but the impression was that it did not impinge more than was strictly necessary. His official briefs from Tanucci,[12] though no doubt extremely bland for reasons of security as they were not written in code, were no more than exhortation to make himself liked by the king and the princesses, as well as the ministers and the ambassadors of important foreign powers, and to keep himself informed about issues and policies that affected the Two Sicilies. And an analysis of the weekly reports of Galiani to Tanucci while he was the embassy's secretary between May 1759 and November 1764[13] comes over more as an exchange of interesting information than the exercise of diplomacy; it must be remembered, however, that Galiani was not the ambassador. One basic reason, which applied equally to Caracciolo's status in Turin and London, was that the Kingdom of the Two Sicilies was not a major power and did not therefore have a huge diplomatic role to play in the vital political and military struggles that were engaging France, Britain, Spain, Austria, Prussia and Russia. The second reason was that, although the king in Naples was a Bourbon Hapsburg and there was theoretically a family pact in existence whereby all Hapsburg royal families declared they would act in alliance, it was Tanucci's policy as principal minister of the Two Sicilies not to honour this when it came to foreign affairs: he was afraid of getting involved in the wars of France or Spain. That was, incidentally, the reason why Galiani was no longer in Paris: on 6 May 1769 Tanucci recalled him to Naples because he had been overheard by one of the foreign minister's, Choiseul's, spies telling the Danish ambassador that the king of Naples would never accede to a family pact; this was reported not to Naples but direct to Spain, and Galiani had to go.[14] Clearly, Caracciolo had little scope diplomatically.

Much of Caracciolo's early work was, as it had been in England, commercial in nature and equally unsatisfactory. He was involved in negotiating a commercial consular treaty with France, which became involved with petty rivalries with England and the old problem of whether Spanish treaties were binding on the Two Sicilies. The troubles first surfaced when Tanucci reported to the king of Spain (he always kept him informed, right up till his death) on 9 June 1772[15] that the king of the Two Sicilies had been upset to read a letter from Caracciolo explaining that the French naval secretary had been creating problems about matters concerning consuls and commerce that, according to his previous letters, had already been agreed and only needed copying and signing. Caracciolo had not specified what the problems were, but he would, he said, be sending a memorandum on the subject. Tanucci's next letter[16] explains that though the

French minister was in favour of the treaty as it stood (the Two Sicilies' commerce with France could be equal), the English were not prepared to give any of their advantages away, and the French could not disadvantage themselves *vis à vis* the English. Caracciolo talked of the friction between the Spanish and the French; Tanucci reiterated that the Two Sicilies were bound by no Spanish treaties.

By September Caracciolo had found an earlier Spanish treaty with France that he thought would simplify everything and he proposed it as a solution.[17] This proved optimistic, and by December 1772 Caracciolo was so fed up with the whole business that he was proposing that no consuls should be received from either France or Britain and that the only Sicilian consul, who was in Marseilles, should be recalled. If the king were to agree, a reasoned document would then be drawn up to illustrate how badly the negotiations had been conducted.[18] By January the French were complaining they could not sign because their consuls would not have plenipotentiary rights, which had been cancelled when the *Magistrato del Commercio* had been set up, so once again Caracciolo was advising his king to forget about the whole business.[19] He did try again with the earlier Spanish treaty but he complained that the French completely misunderstood it: anyway, nothing came of it. Although he was considered an economist, Caracciolo was not a successful negotiator of commercial treaties.

Somewhat more swashbuckling was the attempt to take over the small island of Lampedusa, south of Sicily – an attempt Caracciolo helped to thwart from far away in Paris. The prince of Lampedusa had let his small island to a Frenchman who with an unruly company of Maltese under some sort of protection from the French minister on Malta (to which the island is quite close) and safe conducts from North Africa was apparently cultivating the island. The French minister on Malta denied issuing safe conducts and stated that according to him the people on Lampedusa were Maltese, whereupon the Maltese ambassador in Paris formally demanded either rent for Lampedusa or money from the sale of the island. All this was discovered by Caracciolo at Paris and reported by him to the Neapolitan court.[20] By the end of the year he was following this information up with practical advice to the king: the Maltese were trying to usurp the island with French protection and the king must make a decisive move. The Maltese must be expelled, a fort built and a garrison installed.[21] By February 1772 Caracciolo had gained even better information: he now knew that the Duke of Praslin had been involved with the French minister in Malta as long ago as the days of the regency in infiltrating the island of Lampedusa. There had been talk in the past of putting up a fort, but nothing had been done about it. There were some North African firmans for the odd Maltese to do some agriculture, but nothing of note. The government should note, said Caracciolo, that this was not a viable economic project, but a fortress should be built for reasons of decorum (rather like the project on the island of Ventotene). This would cost about 30,000 *ducati*, but he thought it ought to be done. Incidentally, Tanucci actually asked for the King of Spain's opinion.[22] To this day there is no fortress on Lampedusa, but the island is still Italian.

Other references to Caracciolo in official correspondence tend to be of an ad hoc nature. We see him briefly organising a doctor for the queen's birth in 1771; in the same year he was involved in trying to persuade the government to buy arms for 300,000 ducats not in England but in France, but this was denied due to Tanucci's mercantilist view that since the Two Sicilies had an imbalance of trade with France the arms would have to be paid for in cash, living blood of the state ('*sangue vivo dello stato*').[23] On various occasions he expressed his views on the belligerent intentions of England, presumably as an expert, because he had been ambassador there. He was slightly involved in questions concerning Avignon and Benevento. During the Sicilian corn crisis in 1773 he helped to find provisions in France, but was not gratified by squabbles about payment. Around the middle of the decade the impression was that his official duties were becoming less taxing. Against this one must weigh the fact that in 1775 the king awarded Caracciolo the Order of San Gennaro, an honour by no means lightly doled out by the monarch and much prized by its recipients.

Other letters to Galiani around this time deal with literary and anti-clerical matters. In March 1772 he was discussing the six-volume *Istoria filosofica e politica del commercio e dello stabilimento degli europei nelle due Indie* (*Philosophical and political history of the commerce and the establishment of Europeans in the two Indies*), which had been published anonymously, surreptitiously and without a licence: it was the talk of all Paris and rumour (correctly) had it that the author was the Abbé Raynal. In the same letter Caracciolo mentions that he had been defending one of his early intellectual mentors, the Neapolitan philosopher Giannone, before a minister in a fight with the bishops. More mundanely, he was also trying to obtain special testimonials (without success, however) from the new French foreign minister the Duc d'Aiguillon for Galiani, who was at the time apparently contemplating settling down in Naples. His letters on this matter dovetailed into a disagreement between the two friends on economics.

Galiani had published his *Dialogues sur le commerce des blés* (*Dialogues on the commerce of corn*) in 1770 as an attack on the free export of corn; it had at first been greeted with great acclaim, though the 'economists', the Physiocrats or *laissez-faireists*, were decidedly contrary. Galiani was not wholly dogmatic in his argument, allowing that circumstances, times and different countries should have their influence on policy. The result was that, though it was praised by such as Catherine the Great, Diderot and Voltaire, the Physiocrats were constantly against its theory and official acceptance was fluctuating. Caracciolo, in a period during which official thinking was decidedly against any interference with free trade, wrote on 12 June 1773 'Those blessed *Dialogues* on the liberty of exports have done you incredible harm in this country' and described how there was an almost sectarian hatred of his book in Paris. And in a fragment of a letter from a slightly later date, he writes:

> M. Turgot and abbé Morellet maintain that no book had done so much damage to France as your *Dialogues* ... You say that your grain system has not been understood here or people have not wanted to understand it. I tell you what they tell me about the system. Besides, I must not decide if you are right or wrong, because one should examine your book profoundly, which I am reluctant to do at the moment, and then my approval is not worth anything.

Despite possible elements of badinage in this letter, Galiani was rather hurt for a time, but what makes the incident interesting, apart from the momentary misunderstanding between the two friends, was that the government of the grain trade was the subject of Caracciolo's only published work later on in 1785 (*Riflessioni su L'Economia e L'Estrazione de' Frumenti della Sicilia*), in which he too was reconsidering the merits of free trade versus government intervention.

After the death of Louis XV in May 1774 Caracciolo was able to carry out a planned visit to Naples. He arrived in Genoa at the beginning of July as guest of the banker Pietro Paolo Celesia,[24] through whose letters one is able to trace the rather mysterious turbulence that he met with when he got to Naples. The details are not clear, but the fact is that on 3 July 1774 he was having to defend himself from serious attacks from various enemies who wished to deprive him of his post for some recent gaffe that he had committed. Who these people were and what the faux pas was are not known, but the crisis was genuine and, apart from his own self-defence, Galiani was also staunchly engaged on the side on his friend. The fact that Caracciolo had made a howler was nothing new; despite his long years in diplomacy, he was well known for his often surprisingly un-diplomatic use of language. For example, he had said of a prince of the blood in a Paris salon, 'Monsieur le Duc d'Orléons being unable to make Madame de Montesson Duchesse d'Orléons made himself monsieur de Montesson', described Louis XVI's ministers as 'the king's milk teeth' and provoked a printed protest from the physiocrats to the effect that both in France and in Italy a remark he had made about the relations between Marie Antoinette and Turgot 'did much harm to the reputation for discretion that an ambassador should sustain when talking of the affairs of sovereigns'. On another occasion, involving the pope, the king of Naples and even Tanucci, he stated that had he been chief minister of his king he would have soon liberated him from 'the Grand Mufti of Rome'.[25] However, his self-defence and Galiani's support worked in the end, and by August the storm had blown over.

Caracciolo was never fond of Neapolitan society and was now very ready to get back to his beloved Paris. He was, however, prevented by, of all things, the state of his legs. They became bent and swollen and he became obsessed with finding a cure. Paris was postponed and he submitted himself to a frenzy of remedies – sea bathing, steam baths, mineral baths and a whole series of others, among which Galiani noticed little mention of eating sparingly, which was the only really effective one. The period of cure was long and boring, made bearable by his friendship for Galiani. They met ritualistically every Friday when, over an excellent meal, they opened and read to each other the much-longed-for '*lettres de France*'. For Galiani, these came from Madame d'Epinay, for Caracciolo from Mademoiselle Lespinasse, from Chastellux and from other common friends. As Galiani wrote to D'Epinay: 'Thus we communicated to each other our treasures', and then, after lunch, 'we talked tete à tete for two hours at least about Paris'.[26]

But the time was passing and Caracciolo's legs were not getting any better despite treatments that were bordering on the hypochondriacal, so he was forced to hobble to France in time for the consecration of Louis XVI at Rheims on 11 June 1775. Back in Paris, after he attended at court, Madame du Deffant gave a depressing picture of him with his swollen legs (the problem appears to have been dropsy), involving fearful expectorating and cavernous coughing,[27] alleviated only by his famous bonhomie, which soon re-established the atmosphere of jokes and *bons mots* that usually accompanied him in Paris. His jokes and sayings went the rounds and were quoted in various memoirs of the period. Talking of laughter, in September of that year, Galiani wrote to Madame d'Epinay to say that he was writing an *opera buffa*, which was to be versified by Giambattista Lorenzi, have music by Paisiello and be called *Il Socrate Immaginario*: '[W]hen the piece is printed I'll send it to Caracciolo, and he'll undertake to explain its language and humour, and you'll find yourself laughing.'[28]

It was at this point that he became involved in a famous musical *querelle*, between the musical merits of the Austrian–French and the Neapolitan schools in the persons of Gluck and Piccinni, championed in the early stages by Queen Marie Antoinette and Caracciolo respectively. The success of Piccinni's opera *Didone* in Naples led Caracciolo to invite Piccinni to transfer to Paris, offering him a fabulous contract, magnificent lodgings and everything else to match. What seems to have happened can be traced in Marmontel's *Memoires*:

Under the fire king [Louis XV], the Neapolitan Ambassador
had persuaded the Court to get a talented musician to come
from Italy and rebuild the French Opéra which had, for some
time, been showing signs of going to ruin and which was being
kept afloat with difficulty at the expense of the public purse.
The new mistress, Madame du Barry, espoused this idea; and
our Ambassador at the Court of Naples, Baron de Breteuil,
was charged with negotiating the engagement of Piccinni to
come to settle in France, with an annual gratification of two
thousand écus, on condition that he would give us French
operas. As soon as he arrived, my friend the Neapolitan
Ambassador, Marquis Caracciolo, came to me to recommend
and urge me to do for him in Grand Opéra what I had done for
Grétry in Opéra Comique.[29]

The problem was that, on the death of Louis XV (10 May 1774),
Piccinni would find himself the protégé of Madame du Barry, but
subject to Queen Marie Antoinette, whose brother, the Emperor
Leopold, had already warmly recommended Gluck as court
composer. The ingenuous Piccinni arrived 31 December 1776
with his wife and eldest son, but without a word of French or
indeed a penny to his name, and it seems nothing had been done
about the contract or their lodgings. He and his family had to
find space in the Neapolitan ambassador's establishment at the
outset. Madame d'Epinay complained quite bitterly to Galiani
that Caracciolo had done absolutely nothing for the poor
composer.[30] As things began to sort themselves out, Piccinni
began work, with Marmontel as librettist, on the tragic opera
Roland (1778), the first of a series of his Italian operas championed
against those of Gluck, over which 'tout Paris' was split in
polemics that lasted at least until Piccinni finally left the city in
1791. There were successes and failures, scandals, proclamations,
libels and gossip of all sorts. Gluck even wrote to the *Journal del*

Paris to say that he too had written a *Roland*, but had torn it up because it would have been useless to have had it produced, seeing the 'protection' that the Italian version enjoyed. Caracciolo, of course, was involved only in the early stages, as he was soon called away to other shores.

Before being called away, however, he got into a scrape of another kind, despite his 65 years and the fact he was suffering from dropsy. As already mentioned, he was in the habit of acquiring his love life on an ad hoc basis, and in 1780 he had a particularly warm affair with a pretty young Greek girl from Corfu who was in Paris, only to discover that he had contracted symptoms that made medical intervention necessary.[31]

Then came a bolt from the blue. In May 1780 he learnt, to his horror, that he had been appointed Viceroy of Sicily. As early as 8 March 1772 he had written to Galiani: 'I have fixed my soul on passing the remainder of my days in Paris.' So it was hardly surprising that his reactions to the promotion were negative in the extreme.

At first he shut himself up and refused to see anybody, according to his friend Celesia,[32] and then he exaggerated in visits. Always late in taking up new appointments, this was his record: he managed to put off taking official leave of the French court until 17 April 1781. When the moment arrived there was a beautiful official exchange of niceties between Louis XVI and ambassador Caracciolo: '*Vous allez occuper, Monsieur, une des plus belles places d'Europe*'; '*Hélas! Sire, la plus belle place de l'Europe est celle que je quitte: c'est la place de Vendome!*'[33]

Part Two

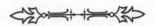

Intermezzo

5

Why was Caracciolo the Choice?

❧

O ne has to step back slightly to appreciate why the court at Naples considered Caracciolo the only real candidate for the viceregency of Sicily in 1780. They clearly wanted him, as he did not deign to arrive in Palermo until 13 months after the royal appointment. They tolerated the delay in his taking up the post and he retained his ambassadorial salary during all those months of dithering and bemoaning the fact that he was being torn from his beloved Paris. The background to the decision to appoint him is quite complex: it involves local, national and international politics and evolved over a considerable period of time.

In 1734 in the *Codice di Melfi*, King Charles (previously the Duke of Parma) set out the terms of his becoming the king of both Naples and Sicily. He became monarch of both, but chose to reside in Naples (a fact that offended the Sicilians, who considered themselves the senior kingdom and Palermo the natural location for the court, in contrast with the Neapolitans, who considered themselves on much higher historical, cultural and political ground than the Sicilians). The *Codice* recognised that both countries had their own constitutions and ancient traditions, which were grounds for major problems of government right up until 1860, when Garibaldi succeeded in formally uniting the separate Italian territories into a single Kingdom of Italy. Sicily was particularly jealous of its constitution, its *Parlamento* (which was frequently compared to Westminster) and its ancient traditions, which were inviolable. Sicily was to be administered, however, by the king through a viceroy, with limited powers, located in Palermo. Charles, while he ruled the Two Kingdoms together with his trusted Tuscan prime minister, Tanucci, was able to carry out quite a number of significant reforms in Naples as a small Enlightened despot – that is to say, reforms were conceived and executed in the name of the king alone without wide consultation. The king, however, needed taxes from Sicily, which by constitution and custom were only granted by the Sicilian *Parlamento* (they were, in fact defined as 'donations', occasional and not permanent due taxes, a usage jealously guarded by the Sicilians). So the tendency in Naples was to leave Sicily alone, because the constitutional, legal and political problems that would have had to be faced if serious reforms were to be undertaken there were judged too difficult and indeed dangerous. Even though Naples had the advantage culturally (it was known internationally as having probably the most ancient university in Europe, where Genovesi and Giannone taught, whereas Sicily was known internationally for Cagliostro and the education there was almost entirely in the hands of the Jesuits), Palermo had an ancient constitution, time-honoured privileges and ever-present thoughts of independence.

Tanucci held the reins of government from 1734 to 1776, carrying out what Enlightened reforms he was able to in Naples, but leaving Sicily to its own devices to avoid stirring up a potential hornets' nest. He continued, in fact, the Spanish world-wide Bourbon policy of ruling through viceroys, who were left alone as long as enough money came back home.

When the king in southern Italy became Charles III of Spain in 1759 he continued to exert considerable influence on his former Italian territories through Tanucci, as we have seen. He left behind his nine-year-old son Ferdinando as king in Naples and Palermo, although in the hands of a regency consisting of Neapolitans and Sicilians, and his education in those of the Prince of Sannicando, well known for his personal ignorance and his defence of this in general.[1] The result was that the boy king grew up also ignorant and with little encouragement to learn the trade of kingship. In his lifetime he was chiefly known for his excessive love of the hunt and the table, though he did show a certain interest in ecclesiastical matters.

Tanucci in Naples was able to achieve one major reform that included Sicily – the abolition of the Jesuits, whose order had been dissolved by Pope Clement IV in 1773. In Sicily, as well as controlling the educational system, they had money, and 40,000 hectares of land. Tanucci also organised the redistribution of much of this land among the peasants, arranging bridge financing and following Genovesi's principle of *'livellate, livellate, ma a piccoli porzioni'* ('level, level, but in small portions').[2] The initial results were successful, and Tanucci also used the Jesuit cash that had been accumulated to create a series of lay, state, free schools, again following Genovesi's teaching that education was a public right. The number of schools was limited by the availability of the funds that became available, but this was an innovative step. Genovesi was, as we have seen, a guiding light for Caracciolo since his earliest days. The then Viceroy of Sicily, Fogliani, was not in favour of these reforms, but he himself was forced to flee from his office later on in 1773 by a dangerous, apparently popular, revolt ostensibly brought about by the trade guilds, but with the heavy backing of the Sicilian barons on the sidelines. The revolt was a serious one and was not forgotten for many a long year in Naples: it underlined the differences in the two kingdoms, the difference of the constitutional situation, the power of the barons, the weakness of the viceroy (and therefore the king) and the fierce sense of independence that the Sicilians (barons, of course) felt.

As the young king grew up and was married to Maria Carolina, the daughter of the Austrian Empress Maria Theresa (and therefore sister to the more famous Marie Antionette), a new element to his rule gradually gained ground. His queen enjoyed, by marriage contract, the right to participate in the rule of the two kingdoms through her membership of the *Consiglio di Stato*[3]; she made her presence felt and a growing tendency towards a new foreign policy became evident. The aim was to detach the two Italian kingdoms from the hitherto heavy influence of Charles III of Spain (as we have seen in the correspondence already considered) and to re-align their policies with those of Austria, the major power in Italy at that moment. The elements that led to this change were the king's growing 'maturity', which involved a natural desire to relinquish his dependence on his father, and his queen's growing, but natural, desire to move her new country's policies into the orbit of her native country. As the pressure grew, a plot to get rid of Prime Minister Tanucci began to foment. The queen was obviously involved, as was the Sicilian Marquis of Sambuca, at the time the ambassador at Vienna. The result was that Tanucci was ousted in 1776 and the court found itself obliged to find a successor. There were two choices: Caracciolo or Sambuca. The situation and how it was resolved was neatly captured by Luigi dei Medici, a jurist, future prime minister and first-hand witness:[4]

As soon as the conspirators against Tanucci believed that they were safe with the King of Spain's agreement for his removal, they began to dispute as to who should be the successor. The majority was for Caracciolo, the Ambassador to France, a gentleman of exquisite intellect and more than adequately well read, but those who frequented the Queen wanted the choice to fall on the Marquis Sambuca, our Ambassador to Vienna, and it was said that His Catholic Majesty was consulted, who considering Caracciolo a free man and one of little religion gave his preference to the other.

It must also be said that the presence of Sambuca as ambassador in Vienna must have been a sign of general queenly approval, but probably the rumoured intervention of Charles III of Spain against Caracciolo as a friend of Voltaire as well as Caracciolo's failure to visit Vienna on his way back to Paris after a brief visit to Naples in 1775 (which irked the queen) were also factors. He was also known as a friend of Tanucci's.

Sambuca remained in power as prime minister for ten years, from 1776 till 1786. In 1788 Admiral Sir John Acton was co-opted from Tuscany as minister of marine affairs and soon had the ear (and perhaps more) of the queen. They became, in fact, the ruling partnership. This diminished Sambuca's influence in some respects, but he still enjoyed a great deal of power in his sector, particularly in Sicilian affairs. Both the queen's close alliance with Acton and the preferences of Sambuca himself (who was essentially a conservative) brought about the end of any sort of Enlightened despotism that had been associated with Tanucci. Sambuca's permanence in power was a great deal less dignified than his predecessor's. He stamped on Tanucci's socially considerate policy of dealing with the confiscated Jesuit property in Sicily and procured for himself and his friends directly or indirectly enormous tracts of their land there, not honouring the existing contracts with the peasants and/or forcing them out of possession.

The Spanish influence in Sicily was, however, despite the change of royal policy, still strong. The island's pride in its *Parlamento*, the *Capitoli del Regno* (codified traditions) and even the *Codice di Melfi* was growing, and abuses were being consolidated – the *Deputazione del Regno*, which should have by constitution represented all three branches of *Parlement* and overseen general policy, was by this time entirely dominated by the barons. With the ever-present recollection of the dangerous 1773 Sicilian revolt in the court's mind, the realisation that Sambuca had reneged on his anti-Spanish policy and the fact that the barons of Sicily were obviously pro-Spanish by tradition and open to leadership by Sambuca (as well as the fact that Viceroy Stigliano, Fogliani's successor, was coming to the end of his stint in office), it was clear that something serious had to be done. It might be added that there was evidence that Caracciolo was sympathetic to Emperor Joseph's later reforms, which might have influenced the queen, his sister.

The above is, in short, the background to the queen's and Acton's decision to move Caracciolo from Paris to the post of Viceroy of Sicily. This was essentially a move to balance the influence of Sambuca: Spain still exercised some influence in the two kingdoms and Sambuca had clearly turned from the anti-Spanish position he held during the plot to get rid of Tanucci. The aristocrats, who had much more power in Sicily than in Naples, were mostly for the Spanish traditions; the masons (Caracciolo was one, and they were much more influential in Naples than Sicily) were more inclined to Vienna. He was also and evidently not an ambitious man as far as his career was concerned and had not been taken up with the Neapolitan kingdom's politics, whereas Sambuca was and had been. Sambuca, son of the Prince of Camporeale, was an obvious candidate for baronial leadership in Sicily and Naples was always mindful of the aforementioned 1773 revolt. Caracciolo's loyalty to the monarchy was well known. The royal decision was communicated by Sambuca, although he could hardly have been happy with it. Neither was Caracciolo.

Caracciolo was quite elderly by then and enjoying a most satisfying life in Paris, where he was honoured and courted. As early as 8 March 1772 he had written to Galiani: 'I have fixed my soul on passing the remainder of my days in Paris.' His next move, he thought, would be retirement with a suitable pension from the king after his long, loyal service. Although by now more an international figure than a Neapolitan, he shared that country's undervaluation of Sicily's circumstances, many rungs below Naples culturally and politically. He also knew that unless he continued in the viceregal tradition of shuffling papers and not doing anything of note, the job he as a figure of Enlightenment would have to do would be most difficult and exhausting – he was, after all, an idealist and would be obliged to administer the island according to his principles. Yet he revered the king and felt obedience. He was informed of the royal decision in May 1780, travelled to Naples in June 1781, and only in October of that year went to Palermo. To put it mildly, he was extremely reluctant to take up his appointment. As Galiani wrote to Madame d'Epinay from Naples when his friend arrived: '*Il parle toujours de Paris; mais il vivra loin de Paris*.'⁵

Caracciolo's time in Naples was taken up with briefing himself about this new position. But the court wanted him so much that they were entirely tolerant of his delays and continued to pay him his ambassadorial salary until he was in a position to make up his mind. During his time there he met and established a good relationship with Minister Acton – indeed, he negotiated that he should report to the king through Acton rather than Sambuca (which was the accepted practice, since he was the principal minister). He talked to Tanucci, now retired and off the scene, and all the relevant institutions in Naples that could bring him up to date on the Sicilian situation, particularly the *Giunta di Sicilia*, which spelled out the limitations to viceregal power on the island. It would have been strange if he had not expressed his Enlightenment ideas in legislation, agriculture and social affairs, and therefore how he intended to administer Sicily, but there appears to be no documentation to that effect.

6

What Awaited Him

❧❀❧

This is how Caracciolo described his early impressions on arriving in Sicily to his friend Galiani on 21 December 1781.[1]

Here I am, my dear friend, relegated to the arid shores of savage Sicily, and occupied 'martially' in procuring the public good. But I meet with great difficulties and hindrances at every step, the most troublesome of which probably derive from the defects of the government itself. So many tribunals, so many jurisdictions, so many opposing orders and despatches from different Secretaries, such laxity in discipline and such contempt for the laws would make the Christ at the *Cristo del Carmine* [a church in Naples] throw up His arms. Apart from the fact that the country itself is badly organised. Sicily is inhabited by great lords and miserable folk, that is to say oppressors and oppressed, because those who busy themselves with justice here serve as instruments of oppression ...

Not that he was new to the problems of Sicily. As a mainland Neapolitan he would have shared a general feeling that Naples and its affairs were a cut above Palermo and theirs, a feeling that was reflected in government attitudes in Naples and resented on the island. Much of this attitude of distrust was picked up by such foreign visitors as had the courage to visit what was then widely considered a rather savage, backward, bandit-ridden corner of Europe. These gentlemen may have stayed there for only short periods of time and some (particularly the Scotsman Brydone[2]) did not shy away from some embroidery when describing the environment, but their analyses of the misery in the Sicilian countryside and the disarray of the government ought to be taken into consideration. They went to the island with fresh eyes. In the context of the relations between Naples and Palermo (which was a central problem for Caracciolo in its form of viceregal-versus-baronial rule and the question of separate constitutions) it would be appropriate to quote Comte De Borch, who blamed the tense relationship 'on an innate, so to speak, antipathy between the two peoples', which was the cause of sad consequences on the island, and which 'the Government could easily eliminate if it were to establish more dealings between the two nations'[3] – note that he talked of 'two nations'. More succinctly, the author of *Lettres sur L'Italie en 1785* had this to say:

> The Sicilians are looked on as foreigners in Naples; at Court as enemies. It is believed that to vex them is to govern them; to make them subject slaves is to make them faithful subjects. In a word, The Ministry looks upon Sicily as a troublesome appendage: the Court has eyes for Naples only.[4]

Both these and other writers were stressing that mainland Naples and Sicily were worlds apart, though ruled by one king. The fact was that, after a very long period of monarchical absenteeism, Sicily had to all intents and purposes grown into a separatist feudal oligarchy. The barons were quite convinced that their constitution, the origins of which they traced back to Norman times, was the only one in Italy that could boast representative bodies that determined legitimate powers. They further felt that Sicily not only had a better, or rather a more ancient, right than Naples to be a kingdom, but that anyway, *vis à vis* the papacy, it was also an independent one because it enjoyed the papal legacy bestowed in 1068 by Pope Urban II, whereas Naples was merely a tributary state in that it paid homage to Rome through the institution of the *Chinea*. Not only that, Sicily had, over the centuries, developed separate constitutional, legal and administrative systems, which had become its distinct privileges. The first of the many tasks that faced the new viceroy, therefore, was the restoration of the monarchy, an institution that Caracciolo, incidentally, firmly believed in *per se*.

That the land in Sicily belonged to the barons was quite clear, but how, by what rights and with what obligations was not. The only official statistics when Caracciolo arrived were, and are, dicey, to say the least. These go under the name of the *Numerazione* or *Descrizione*, a sort of census-cum-land-survey of 1747–8 that was not even published until 1770.[5] Excluded from the analysis was the city of Palermo, which for tax purposes was arbitrarily calculated at a tenth of the population of the whole island (its population was actually around 180,000 in 1770, which made it the second-largest city in Italy after Naples). Also excluded were the value of all goods situated inside the city of Palermo, the value of goods belonging to its citizens but held outside the city and the value of all goods belonging to all nobles in Palermo or not. These last three items were not surveyed because they were not taxable. From the *Numerazione*, with all its defects, it was apparent that more than two-thirds of the territory of the island and about half of the population (Palermo, remember, was excluded) was 'baronial', that is to say it came under feudal rather than monarchical jurisdiction. But there were no surveys, no registers, no title deeds, no lists of obligations or duties ... an almost total lack of legal documentation.

The state did not know how the island was 'composed' feudally, nor indeed did the feudal owners themselves know much more. One of them, Don Diego Aragona Pignatelli Cortes e Mendoza, the Prince of Castelvetrano, even commissioned a survey of what he owned in Sicily when he inherited in 1725, and the editor of the work (the number and the extent of the properties was such that he had to farm the research out) had to admit in the introduction to his findings that he could not guarantee all of the details for some of the cities, lands and estates because it was not possible to know 'what place in them had played passion, contemplation and connivance'.[6] This confusion as to the true state of affairs also applied to the ecclesiastical organisations, the cities and the towns. The barons were apt to look on their land as a mysterious source of power and prestige that just belonged to them, rather than legally owned wealth. Most *latifondi* (large feudal estates) were collections of separate landholdings with different forms of cultivation including woods and pasture, but mostly the land went uncultivated. Neighbouring lands and towns not originally meant to be legally included became *de facto* incorporated. Jockeying at court and at Palermo, marriages, swapping, marketing, usurpation, buying and selling, stealing and so on all played their part in a long-term policy of consolidation, which was aided and abetted by geographical independence (in other words an almost total lack of roads), and this meant, by the middle of the eighteenth century, that the pattern of land ownership had more or less stabilised. Family interest was uppermost and primogeniture was rigidly enforced. Estates were kept intact because they were *fedecommessi*, i.e. left by will in their entirety to a determined person, usually the eldest son. Land donated to the church was done in *manomorto*, inalienably, and so not subject to succession taxes.

The weakness of the government over the centuries had greatly contributed to the consolidation of this undocumented landholding and by the middle of the eighteenth century the government had little idea if the land was held allodially or feudally, what the legal rights were, where the boundaries lay, what the rights and obligations of the peasants and the townspeople were, whether the towns had been usurped, whether their liberty could be re-acquired, what rights might have been renounced by the peasants for exemption from other burdens or whatsoever. It was a maze of unknowns. In the event of a brave peasant taking a baron to court – a very unlikely event – the poor man would be faced with baron, judge and court in complete cahoots and a total lack of textual evidence. Sicily was firmly in harsh baronial hands, hands that were exempt from paying taxes, safe from legal attacks and immune from state interference.

On the jurisprudence of feudalism itself and its place in the hierarchy of power, the evolution had been slow but consistently in favour of the barons against the monarchy, and against the trend in the rest of Europe. Since Norman times it had been the general rule that feudal estates were inalienable and reverted to the crown when heirs were lacking or relations were intolerable, as expressed in Roger II's *Scire* volumes and Frederick II's *Constutiones divae memoriae*, but Frederick III of Aragon with his 1289 *Volentes* established that feudal property could be freely alienated by its legitimate owners in the hope of thereby weakening the barons. There had also been some confusion about inheritance and reversion because of the existence the two traditions of subdivision (the Lombard tradition) and no-subdivision (the Frankish tradition): this had been sorted out by Frederick II with his *In Aliquibis* and *De successione nobelium in feudis*, but James of Aragon in a bid to bring the barons on to his side issued his *Si aliquam*, which extended inheritance to the sixth-grade collateral and meant that the feudal estates practically never reverted to the state for lack of heirs. The measure was later confirmed by Frederick III and the barons ever afterwards looked on *Si aliquam* and *Volentes* as fundamental privileges. By the first measure their vassalage towards the crown was seriously weakened, and by the second the rights of the exchequer were badly damaged. By 1747, the Sicilian nobles were petitioning for the extension of rights up till the seventh grade.[7]

There was also a serious attempt at redefining the 'feudal contract', which had constitutional implications. The theory can be synthesised as follows: the Norman invasion of Sicily was not a classical feudal invasion because the Great Count Roger's poverty meant that he could not afford to command a feudal army, but was in fact helped by fellow men-at-arms (*commilitones*): after the conquest he did not concede lands in feudal tenure to his followers but divided them up among his friends more in the way of spoils. This theory had obvious implications on the constitutional front and it was used successfully by the lawyer Carlo di Napoli in 1740 in a famous court case concerning the town of Sortino and its eponymous prince, from whom the town unsuccessfully tried to buy its freedom. Such was the satisfaction of the baronage that they erected a marble bust of di Napoli in the senate house in Palermo. Later on, di Napoli was to write:

> a law formed in public Assemblies cannot be violated by others than those who formulated it, and never by the Prince alone, because if he knew he could not have proclaimed it by himself, it is necessary that he accepts the contribution of others in its reformulation, and particularly its repeal.[8]

So there became a stage when the barons, fiercely independent on their own feudal lands, attempted to become the legislating partners of the monarchy in *Parlamento*, a body they looked on as the legitimate representative of the Sicilian people, although it only in fact represented themselves.

One of the few areas where satisfactory reforms were almost achieved in the period before the arrival of Caracciolo (and not exclusively in favour of the barons) concerned the landholdings that became available after the expulsion of the Jesuits in 1767.[9] These lands were the subject of an enormous project of eighteenth-century social reform, administered by Prime Minister Tanucci to a policy drafted by the famous Genovesi who had been the inspiration of Caracciolo's early education as a young man in Naples, against the barons' interest and in favour of the peasantry.

The original plan was that the lands should be divided up and given to the peasants in emphyteusis (long-term leases on low rents with the obligation of land improvement): very much in the back of Tanucci's mind, apart from genuine ethical considerations, were the periodical famines that plagued the peace of the nation, the latest one occurring in 1763. Despite an initial round of early sharp-dealing when the expulsion was first announced, the law seemed to be working reasonably well at the beginning, but soon a separate *Azienda Gesuitica* was set up to look after the Jesuit land affairs in Sicily so that the then viceroy, Fogliani, who was far too close to baronial interests, could or would not interfere with the working of the overall plan. A confirmatory royal despatch on 25 March 1768 reiterated that the land should be parcelled out to the 'people of the country'.

But the *Giunta di Palermo* immediately asked Judge Paternò for a consultancy, which he duly delivered on 2 May 1768, advising against the royal despatch on three grounds: firstly, there were not enough peasants to carry out the reform, secondly, if the reform were to be carried out there would be no labour for the big estates, and thirdly, if the peasants were given land they would simply live off it and would be useless to the state. These findings only resulted in further riling Tanucci and in 1768 the public auctioning began: the large estates were sold off, mostly to barons, priests and *gabellotti* (large tenant farmers), but without too much abuse; many of the smaller parcels went in emphyteusis to the peasants.

The next phase, after 1769, was a much slower process, as the legal difficulties were becoming apparent, the barons were becoming obstreperous, the financial burdens were beginning to surface, and above all the price of corn began to fall and many of the peasants began to have second thoughts about how good the idea was for them. However, around 1773 Tanucci injected new enthusiasm into the scheme, encouraged by the expulsion of Viceroy Fogliani by the rioting crowds of Palermo, and between 1774 and 1776 most of the remaining emphyteusis packages had been settled. This was not, however, a complete success: peasant debt and bad economic conditions meant that much of the land was repossessed and, after Tanucci's fall in 1776 and the arrival of the Sicilian Marquis Sambuca in power in Naples as prime minister, the tide turned against the peasants and the policy of emphyteusis; the *Azienda Gesuitica* was abolished and peasants were bought or thrown out by Sambuca and his friends. Sambuca did not manage to destroy everything that Tanucci had achieved by any means, but what had been a major piece of social reform had been severely damaged.

When it came to the jurisprudence that was tried in the courts of law, a dim theory of the past had become translated into a welter of confusion and chaos. The theory was the ancient Norman–Hohenstaufen constitution based on the barons' interpretation of the Sicilian *Parlamento* and on the *Capitoli* (the series of edicts such as *Si Aliquam* and *Volentes*) were sacrosanct: an attack on any aspect of these 'privileges' was considered an attack on Sicily itself. Confusion reigned even at this level and in 1784 the Prince of Pantelleria had gone so far as to maintain that Sicilian barons were all hereditary magistrates of the tribunal of the *Gran Corte*.[10] There was no overall view of the situation and no concept that the state had any ethical control. The state was absent, the barons were exercising their power at will, the Spanish had done nothing for centuries other than mollify them, and the field was theirs.

On the mainland the Spanish had at least done something to create a central power, which had debilitated the nobles and cleared the ground for the future Charles III and his son Ferdinand (with the help of Tanucci) to work their reforms, but almost nothing was done in Sicily and its judicial system was left to trundle on as it always had. The result was that peripheral organisations waxed in importance in Sicily as the central ones waned, and the collaboration of *Parlamento* and the barons became essential for any normal viceroy (Count d'Olivares' famous advice to viceroys was 'With the barons you are everything, without them nothing!'[11]).

As far as legislation was concerned, abundance and confusion are the key words: from the Romans to the Austrians, the many conquerors had littered the Sicilian statute books with their own peculiar laws and no attempt had been made to thin them out or codify them. Clearly a great many of them were necessarily contradictory and they could be gleefully used by a good lawyer to distort the cause of 'justice'. Apart from this plethora of legislation, there was also a formidable undergrowth of jurisdictions to be contended with. Every sort of organisation had its own courts, the confines of which were jealously guarded – there was a whole series of ecclesiastical courts, feudal courts, state courts, commercial courts and, of course, myriads of categorical immunities from each of them. The magistrates were notoriously close to the barons, on whom they depended, so it was quite natural that the records reveal a surprising number of appeals against 'suspected' judges. There were official protests to Naples[12] to the effect that, first, it was not possible to obtain written sentences, secondly, the courts should not insist on useless duplication of documents that caused endless delays in justice, thirdly, that they should know the limits of their jurisdictions and so avoid years of wasted time and, fourthly, that they should not take bribes.

The presidents of the various courts were normally barons, who used their considerable influence to the detriment of justice. Although there were no set rules for choosing judges, they usually came from the ranks of the lawyers. The laws they administered were, as has been stated, extremely varied, and up until the time of Caracciolo all new royal decrees (as they did in Spanish times) included an appeal to past laws that may have been forgotten or ignored, evidence no doubt of both conservatism and lack of application. In practice, the magistrates did very much what they wanted and, indeed, often assumed the stature of the legislator in their sentences. Good laws may have existed, but it did not mean that they would necessarily be applied. Any patrimonial case will show how cumbersome Sicilian law was in the application: if there was any sort of feudal connection – and we have already seen that two thirds of Sicily was feudal – it had to be tried by a special feudal procedure, the consequence of which was that three uniform sentences were required from three different courts before the case could be resolved. Moreover, if the case involved the contested ownership of a feudal property, then the procedure was even more complex, because the case could be exported to the mainland and take considerably more time.[13]

The lawyers came from the privileged classes and some of them were even younger sons of the nobility. Their clients were narrow-minded, anti-intellectual and bound to the barons – the opposite of their Neapolitan colleagues (the so-called *Pagliette*, who had been useful in the fight against feudal privilege on the mainland, and had formed a fairly progressive intellectual class that was even slightly politically active). Caracciolo, who it must be remembered had been a judge in Naples, had this to say of

Sicilian lawyers to his friend Galiani in a letter from Palermo on 20 December 1781, soon after his arrival:

> [T]he people of the courts here serve as instruments of oppression ... apart from a great defect in the procedure itself of the tribunals, the biannual magistrature renders the judges pensioners and salaried workers of the barons, because from lawyers they become judges and then pass back to being lawyers: furthermore the ignorance of the legal profession here is superlative: they are all barbarians, perfect barbarians, only one or two of them know the Latin classical authors and no one of them could be described as an expert on questions of law because none of these men of law see or know anything beyond the rites of King Alfonso which is the totality of Sicilian jurisprudence. The Pope of the Sicilian legal scene is president Airoldi, barbarous and ignorant like all the others, but astute, supple, immoral, indifferent to a yes or a no.[14]

So, in a Europe that was generally aiming at centralising and bolstering the power of the state, Caracciolo was faced with a Sicily based on an artificially created, decentralised, baronial 'constitution' and kept in place by 'privileges' defended unjustly in ill-regulated courts.

Leaving legal matters for the economic, specifically agricultural (for the economy of Sicily was almost entirely agricultural), the situation in the sixteenth and until the end of the seventeenth centuries was more or less satisfactory, because the *latifondi*, the large feudal estates, were working well after the anarchism of the previous centuries. New villages were being set up, with civic rights for the peasants, acceptable work contracts, housing and some roads and even some emphyteusis landholdings. After the troubles the barons had returned to their lands and had stayed on them: the peasants were not too badly off and the barons themselves were doing quite well – corn was exported, and even the government profited. By the second half of the eighteenth century, however, the picture was vastly different, the main reason being that the barons had abandoned the country for Palermo, a move that impoverished both the barons and Sicily. As the Frenchman Saint-Non wrote in 1785, the barons of Palermo 'ate gluttonously the products of their lands, that they had never visited'.[15]

In Palermo they lived a wasteful life of luxury. Into the breach, as far as the countryside was concerned, stepped a new figure – the *gabellotto*. He would rent the whole of his property from the baron for a period of three to six years in exchange for much welcomed cash. From the baron's point of view, it is easy to see the advantages of dealing with just one tenant, and having ready cash in hand. From the *gabellotto's* point of view, he had *carte blanche*, as nobody was likely to intervene as long as the baron received his money regularly, and on time. The original *gabellotto* was most probably the peasant made good, either through being a commercial intermediary or a money lender. His objective once he had rented an estate from a baron was to squeeze as much money out of it as fast as possible before his contract ran out. The *gabellotto* was not interested in any long-term plans or eventual emphyteusis arrangements that the barons may have negotiated with the peasants previously with a view to improving the land. Generally speaking, agriculture was reduced everywhere to corn and grazing, even though the laws of the land, custom and good sense laid down a crop rotation procedure of three years. Deforestation was rife, swamps re-appeared, depopulation was rampant, the land was over cultivated; add to this the fact that there were far too few roads and what very little commerce that managed to exist was strangled by a tangle of every sort of taxation, local and state, that imagination could devise, and the picture is complete. The abbot Guerra[16] states that two-thirds of Sicily was completely uncultivated and that, in the third that was, the work was carried out with primitive methods and with 'tools of the most profound rudeness'. Fertilisers were unknown, crops were not rotated, and commercialisation of produce was blocked by taxes and monopolies. There was no wealth.

In fact, Sicily was undergoing an economic crisis. Corn production was very spasmodic; speculation allowed for exports some years, but other years called for imports from as far afield as Russia (and we have already seen Caracciolo at work at London in 1764). Cattle were being imported, as was wine; the silk industry was in decline, and such was the lack of capital that payment in kind and barter was widespread.

Since the economy was agricultural, the origin of the crisis has to be sought in agriculture. The position of the tenants of the barons was no better under the *gabellotto* even from the contractual point of view. There was a myriad of obligations to which they were subject, a few of which were as follows. They were to sow, reap, thresh and harvest the corn and grapes belonging to the baron/*gabellotto* without receiving any payment, and to pay for his wine-press, oil-press, corn mill, slaughterhouse and bakery, all of which they were forced to use after they had supplied the necessary raw materials. As well as items like the iron rings for the owner's barrels, the tenants were required to supply, by contract and free of charge, the so-called *carnaggi*, which consisted of corn, fodder, fruit, wine, oil, fruit, cheese and edibles for animals. There was also a considerable number of days when the tenants were required to labour gratuitously on the land cultivated directly by the baron/*gabellotto* when he was sowing or harvesting (or in truth whenever he wanted; the tenants' animals were also at his beck and call), and so on.

Not only were these obligations onerous, but they were strictly imposed even when times were bad and contractual compliance almost impossible, and there were even cases where the tenants had their properties attacked and were thrown into prison. There were, unsurprisingly, tenants who reverted to being just plain labourers and the plight of the agricultural workers in general was pitiable, a situation reflected in the writings of foreign visitors to Sicily at the time. The result was that Sicily, although it was recognised as one of the most fertile regions of Italy, often did not produce enough to eat. The existence of the *latifondo* had not allowed the rise of the smallholder and the lack of capital had left large properties to drift into the hands of the *gabellotto*, who strangled them in the interests of short-term gain, resulting in terrible social conditions, almost no trade not in foreign hands and such as there was smothered by a mass of disabling taxation.

Meanwhile, the barons themselves were on the verge of bankruptcy even if they were not aware of this. They had debts everywhere – with religious organisations, with money lenders, municipal banks, *monti di pieta* (the mediaeval institutions that were the origins of Italian banking system), cobblers, businessmen, *gabellotti*, hospitals, tradesmen. Even the best of families were in the worst of straits and many of their estates were being administered by the *Deputazione degli Stati*, a body set up to take care of aristocratic families in grave financial circumstances. The barons, however, were always in a position to postpone payment, primarily because they were barons, but more importantly because the whole of the economy would have come crashing down had they been allowed to fail, since it depended on them.

Caracciolo thought otherwise when he wrote to Acton on 2 March 1783 *à propos* of one of these indebted gentlemen:

The Prince of Cattolica has obtained a six month postponement in payment of his debts; here the poor creditors are crying blood: Excellent Sir, the Grocers, the Monks, the

Artisans, the Market Sellers, those who live solely on a subsistence income of 15 scudi, what will they do for six months? There is also the Hospital, how will it look after the sick? In justice the King cannot make use of other people's purses in favour of one rich gentleman, or rather one rich nobody; but these postponements are only obtained by gentlemen in Sicily, not certainly by the poor who are sent to prison without pity, and I say in Sicily because in no other part does one obtain a similar Grace from government; if a debtor has motives for seeking postponement he should be examined and Justice produced. Your Excellency should ask yourself if a similar thing is done in any other part of the world? Is it done in Naples? Why is it only done in Sicily? And why is it only done for important gentlemen? There is nobody crying at the foot of the throne: because the poor man, the widow, the orphan and the hospital have not the means to go to Naples: if a similar injury had been inflicted on a baron he would have shouted to the heavens: 'Justice, Justice'.[17]

There was no middle class preparing to take over from the barons because there was no industry, or commerce to speak of, to give rise to them, and the *gabellotti*, who did have the money, were too busy aping the barons to be a threat to them classwise. The legal middle class, as we have noted, were too dependent on their aristocratic clients. The proletariat, 90 per cent of the population, normally had 0 per cent of public attention and were afraid of protesting their condition, except when the price of food went out of control and then there was rioting and the government became decidedly attentive, as in 1763–4 and 1773.

Perhaps the viceroy's major responsibility was the control of the weight and the price of bread in Palermo, the population of which was rising faster in the eighteenth century than the economy could keep pace with. The main instrument of control was the *Colonna Frumentaria*, a fund established in 1683 to buy corn on the market at any price and sell to the population at a political one. It had a very chequered history, sometimes appearing to work according to the statutes satisfactorily and without mishaps, but sometimes the object of financial raids from all quarters, which depleted its capital (which should have been steady at 100,000 *scudi* to buy corn at harvest time). As time went on, however, maladministration crept in, and after a long series of incidents it was discovered in 1747 that the official bakers (mostly Milanese) had been defrauding the *Colonna* by six *tari* every *salma* of corn for a period of about 40 years. A group of Palermo bakers came forward, made a bid to take over the situation and were granted credit for a large amount of corn, which, when the time came to settle up, they could not pay for, so they took refuge in churches and declared themselves bankrupt (another privilege of the time). In the meantime, the bread had lost weight and quality, and the Milanese had to be taken back even if they were only able to pay two of the six *tari* they owed (the Palermitans did not pay their credit back either).[18] Clearly, administration of this extremely sensitive organisation was not working well. In 1764, the year after the famine (the year Caracciolo was buying corn in London and when everybody was afraid that riots might break out), times were still hard, and Viceroy Fogliani sent parties to scour the countryside looking for hidden corn. This bad year cost the *Colonna* anything from 47,000–56,000 ounces, according to the conservative aristocratic diarist Villabianca. In 1765 it showed a profit of 11,000 ounces, the next year a loss of 9,000, and its capital was reduced to 20,000 ounces in corn and 4,000 in capital. In 1766 it was voted 60,000 ounces and measures were taken to cut down on fraud, but the next two years brought bad losses.[19] This was not just run-of-the-mill inefficiency, but the sort that could bring down governments. In fact, so parlous was the situation that Fogliani turned to unusual taxes to find the necessary money, and his taxes on apertures, balconies and windows, together with his own perceived involvement in unclear dealings, were so unpopular that they lead to his political downfall in 1773. Here again was an area – the administration of food (which meant bread) – in urgent need of reform.

The disastrous effects of the withdrawal of baronial life from the country to the capital were bleak in the extreme, but they were more than made up for in outward appearances by the pyrotechnic shows put on by the barons in Palermo, all of them standing on their rank and title. At the time there were 142 princes, 95 dukes, 788 marquises, 95 counts and 1,275 barons, without calculating the numberless persons using noble titles abusively. Many nobles had more than one title and some had no title at all (as was the case with Caracciolo in Naples before his brother passed him the marquisate to help him out in his career). Their lives were of great external elegance, competitive to extremes and extraordinarily superficial. Appearances were everything, and they cost an eye and a tooth, which the rented estates somewhere in the country simply could not pay for (not that this seemed to matter). This insistence on appearances took on somewhat pathetic aspects, as we can read in Brydone's book when he describes how, during Palermo's *Festa* of Santa Rosalia, when all the streets were lighted up and full of people, he only managed with some difficulty to persuade some gentlefolk to leave their house and take a walk with him in the then main street of Cassero if they were preceded by four liveried servants carrying lighted torches.[20] These and suchlike appearances were costly and family finances and younger children may have suffered consequentially, but, *tant pis*, the nobility still had, or thought they had, a role to play.

It was their firm belief that the defence of their privileges and the constitution was the best guarantee of the happiness of

Sicily: tradition must be upheld. Given the political and economic circumstances of the time, these sentiments were not very useful in public office. These were people who in their own feudal courts could put people away by simply stating 'for reasons well known to us' and did more or less as they willed in state offices, but with little sense of state, no sense of economy, great wastage and complete lack of responsibility.

Probably the greatest problem Caracciolo had to face in Sicily was the great wall of insurmountable, centuries-old privileges that he was faced with. Even in the eighteenth century these had been described as an eminently feudal monarchy pervaded and controlled by privilege[21] and the problem was that an outside attack on them was considered an attack on Sicily itself and all it stood for. It has already been seen that the constitution and the *Capitoli* were interpreted in an anti-monarchical sense and that the development of life and government in the countryside under the barons had found an essential independence from central control; much the same could be said for the administration of the church. But around the various establishments in the city, the church and the country – the associations, guilds, brotherhoods, institutions and whatnot – usages had rapidly grown into formal traditions sanctioned by time. Among the odder privileges was one that belonged to Palermo, which allowed the city to peruse all royal and viceregal decrees before their publication to make sure that none of its enormous privileges had been trampled on. There was a tightly controlled situation in the city of Catania, as revealed in this petition to the king in June 1783:

> The city of Catania has always been the most unfortunate, the worst governed and oppressed by this nobility whose aim has been none other than to enrich itself at the cost of the meek people on whom it founded its inheritance ... in short,

the excise taxes, the monopolies, the lots of horrible cruelties and the thieving are the daily bread of these nobles and they get away with it in triumph: *gloriantur in iniquitatibus suis.* If anybody protests against them, one is immediately slandered, persecuted and ruined materially, in honour and in liberty by falsity and arrogance ... In short, it is a little republic, each one guaranteeing the other, despising holy and human laws and even independent of the Sovereign ... The number of the nobility is few and mainly consists of the family of Paternò ... If a just and impartial governor from other parts does not come.[22]

On his own land, if and when he was there – or through his delegates when not – the baron's privileges were awesome. According to one ancient decree, a baron was theoretically a *Capitano di Guerra*, a warlord, but even without such extreme powers he could, for instance, quite easily elect his own officials at will (even if the law might require a ballot), decide not to replace them after a year (as the law dictated), refuse to allow them to undergo the *'sindacato'* (inspection or audit of the service at the end of its term), allow them on the other hand to occupy (illegally) more than one office at a time, and so on. Through these officials, he did more or less what he wanted, manipulating at will documents concerning civic rights, usages, taxes, legal wrangles, etc. Where he had the rights of *'mero e misto impero'* he could make laws, elect judges to apply them and officers to carry out the sentences in his own prisons. The municipal food supply and finance were also in baronial control: his own officials fixed the prices of the commodities in his own interests, inventing and inflicting fines, extortions and sequestrations, controlling weights and measures and feudal taxes, conducting surveys of men and animals, valuing goods, receiving and dividing up payments of taxes in accordance with baronial regulations or local customs. It was also not unusual for baronial organisations to harbour and benefit from bandits under their wings. In this sorry administration the state was more absent than the baron, but the peasant was none the wiser.

The supreme Sicilian privilege was the *Parlamento*. Unlike other representative bodies in other parts of Europe, its existence had not been worn away by the monarchy, but had been left intact to be what it still was by the second half of the eighteenth century – a feudal body. It had indeed lost most of its powers (its elective, legislative and judiciary powers and its ability to inspect and audit public institutions and offices), but it did retain one function, which was its *raison d'être* in the eighteenth century: its exclusive power to vote taxes and to divide the payment of them between the various categories of contributors. It could also make requests (*grazie*) to the king, but these he could refuse. The king could *not* impose taxes, a fact of great importance in Caracciolo's struggle to reform Sicily.

Parlamento consisted of three chambers. The Military or Feudal chamber held 228 baronial members who cast votes for all the towns within the boundaries of their estates (Prince Butera, the hereditary president, for example had no fewer than 41 votes in 1690); they did not need to turn up for discussions if they did not want to, but could delegate anybody they wanted, sometimes even their *gabellotto*. The second, Ecclesiastical, chamber was chaired by the Archbishop of Palermo and consisted of 63 or more bishops and abbots with royal benefices elected by the king: they were highly conservative and when asked for any new tribute invariably asked for papal permission. The third, Demesne, chamber theoretically represented those townships that owed allegiance to the crown rather than a feudal lord, but was presided over by the *praetor* of Palermo, who was a noble, and its members were voted by the municipal administrators and representatives of the craftsmen, both of which relied heavily on the nobility, so many of them turned out to be either barons or their clients. On several occasions viceroys tried to get the Demesne chamber on the government's side by packing it, but even when this happened it was never a 'people's' chamber, nor a chamber that was listened to. *Parlamento* normally met every four years, when it voted the normal taxation without discussion, and usually any abnormal fiscal requests were put forward by the king: the sessions were ceremonious and separate with a solemn plenary session where each chamber voted. In the final session the special requests (the *grazie*) were voted and it was normal that the most voted *grazie* in only one chamber were accepted without appeal, even if they went against the interests of another chamber. Before Caracciolo came on the scene this fossilised system of government had continued unperturbed. It is true that in 1746 the Demesne chamber had protested that the share it had to pay of the taxes voted was unjust, but nothing came of the debate; it is also true that in 1754 the Marquis of Spaccaforno challenged the viceroy over requests for taxes and brought up the issue of the liberty of *Parlamento*, but the taxes passed and he was put in prison for his pains.[23]

As a matter of ancient custom all taxes were voted by *Parlamento* and the share divided between the three chambers, after which it was the task of the *Deputazione del Regno*, the feudal institution *par excellence*, to make the fine calculations on just how the tax would be paid region by region, town by town, based on false census information. After this the local barons or their agents would be sent out to get the money as best they could. The *Deputazione del Regno* administered and collected, with great iniquity and inefficiency, these tributes, which were the only royal income in Sicily, since the king did not own any land: he could not even call the post office his own, as we shall see later on. A further block on Sicilian initiatives or a reforming viceroy was the constitution by Charles III of the so-called *Giunta di Sicilia*, a five-member committee of which the president and two members had to be Sicilian, which sat in Naples, advised the king and effectively stifled all innovations.

At this point it is worth investigating who actually paid these tributes or taxes that *Parlamento* voted and how they were collected. Without going into too much detail, the so-called taxes were actually called 'gifts' (*donativi*), and they were either ordinary or extraordinary. Altogether, there were around 14, worth about 300,000 *tari*; only some 50 per cent went directly to the court. There was also a series of other tributes that had been in origin extraordinary, but had gained ordinary status over the years. This was not considered a heavy fiscal burden on the whole,[24] but what was iniquitous, indeed cruel, was the way the money was collected. For example, the barons paid nothing towards any of the 10 ordinary *donativi*, and only from a quarter to a tenth of the other four. The reason for this was that, right in the middle of the Age of Reason, the barons in Sicily were exempt from paying taxes, stating that they did not even have to pay the ancient *adoa* and *relatio* for the possession of their feudal land, but just had to supply the king with men and horses in time of war according to an antiquated mediaeval table that was still apparently in existence. As far as the ecclesiastics were concerned, the situation was much the same: although they did not contribute men and horses to the king, certain high prelates were completely exempt from all payments, and most of the others paid just a sixth of the total due on the other *donativi* on the basis of incomes declared during the arbitrary period of 1720–30. The cities also had their very own privileges, led by Palermo, which, although by far the richest conglomeration on the whole island, paid just one tenth of each *donativo*; Siracusa, Augusta, Carlentini and Marsala paid for only four of the *donativi*, their contributions towards the others being spread among the other non-feudal towns. There were of course many other exemptions for many other idiosyncratic reasons. The only people not exempt were the 'people', but not even this was simple because the taxes were divided 50:50 between the feudal and demesnial towns, whereas there were actually 282 feudal *università* against just 85 demesnial ones, so the tax burden was exceptionally unfair on the demesne population. The actual collection of the money was entirely arbitrary and without any sort of control.

Perhaps the least appealing aspect of his elevation to the viceroyalty from Caracciolo's personal point of view was the cultural life on the island, for it must be admitted that the intellectual atmosphere of Sicily was sharply different from the *salons* of Paris where he had recently been so pleasantly ensconced. He was bound to miss his *philosophes* friends, though some of the *Encyclopédie*'s references to the island reveal an extraordinary ignorance of it (among many other surprising entries on Sicily, in *Tome* XI [p. 708] it printed that Palermo had been destroyed by an earthquake at a time when it was disputing Messina's title of capital of Sicily, a fact that greatly annoyed the Palermitans). The general intellectual atmosphere was firmly conservative. Official academic culture was still chained to mediaeval scholastic tradition and not openly welcome to any form of Enlightenment. Even if its days were numbered, the Inquisition was still formally in existence, and superstition was rife among the illiterate majority. This did not mean of course that there were no individuals embracing the new teachings. Various historians have written about the late arrival of the new culture in the island, whether it was the reading of Rousseau by society ladies or Tomaso Natale getting away with putting Liebnitz's philosophy into Tuscan verse because he was a gentleman.[25] Francesco Paolo Di Blasi, who would be hanged at the end of the century for conspiring to establish a Republic of

Sicily, was already in 1778 writing on the natural equality of man; Sergio the eminent economist was already at work, as was Rosario di Gregorio the jurisconsult, the writer De Cosmi and the Prince of Biscari and his school of archaeologists. There is no doubt that the works of Locke, Hume, Liebnitz, Wolfe and company were being read in the environs of the *Academia* (which had been founded in 1779 with the proceeds of the expulsion of the Jesuits), and, even if the Archbishop of Palermo in his pastoral instructions of 1770 complained that 'a torrent of dangerous books from ultramontane regions has come to flood us',[26] few would maintain that this culture was anything other than very superficial, the property of a privileged few that did not have any drip-down effect on society as a whole. It is quite easy to understand why Caracciolo did not display any intellectual enthusiasm for his new life.

***

The historical events of the last few years before the arrival of Caracciolo in Sicily highlight many of the problems that have been briefly examined in the previous pages.

They emerge from the long, rather eventless viceregency of the Marquis Giovanni Fogliani di Aragona, formerly the principal minister at Naples, but installed as viceroy on 23 June 1755, who governed for 18 years and was much loved by the barons because he elected not to interfere with them, but rather entertained them in the manner to which they felt accustomed. His biographer Giovanni Battista Di Blasi wrote of him:

> This Viceroy continued to be the delight of the Nation; his sweet manners, his generosity, his charity towards the poor, and above all his soul which was always far removed from novelties which often turn out to be pernicious, attracted to him the love of everybody. Thus everyone made it their duty

to venerate him, nor was there public festivity in the homes of the Nobles to which he was not invited to honour; and when present at parties or dinners he kept the Nobility amused and attached sincerely to him. These recreations which he allowed himself and the Baronage did nothing to prevent him from dedicating himself indefatigably to the cares of government and the procurement of happiness for Sicily.[27]

Fogliani was faced with great problems in 1763 and 1764 with the famine, with the hungry from the country laying siege to Palermo and with trying to shore up the ailing finances of the *Colonna Frumentaria*. He managed to be on the Jesuit side and with the barons against Tanucci after their expulsion after 1767; he reformed the law so that clandestine marriages, which were damaging to the baronage, were made more difficult. It is true he did give the formal start, with Sambuca's collaboration, to the *Academia*, which, with ex-Jesuit money, was to become the nucleus of the university, and a tentative start was made to a public cemetery – both projects that were later close to Caracciolo's heart – but neither came to much fruition under his care. The fact is that during his long viceregency very little was achieved, except keeping the barons happy by not interfering with them. By 1773, however, the situation had become critical: to repair the ailing finances of the *Colonna Frumentaria*, his taxes on windows and balconies, on wine and even on snow (which was used in ice cream and drinks) were badly taken and there were refusals to pay, which was a very worrying sign. Moreover, 1772's had been a bad harvest, the price of bread was rising and there was something more than a whiff of revolt in the air, a situation that would have been much worse had not the Prince of Cassaro been *praetor* (in charge of food affairs in Palermo). Cassaro was an honest man and much respected by the people and when he fell ill everybody was concerned: was he suffering from stones or not, should he be operated or not, what should be done? Fogliani was part of the surgery school and persuaded Cassaro to be operated on by a new surgeon just arrived from France, but the operation went badly and immediately the mob began to blame Fogliani. The saints were brought out and processed in the streets, Fogliani, in panic, announced that Cassaro's brother would be appointed *praetor* if his brother died; the mob was let into the palace to see with their own eyes if he were dead or alive. The craftsmen's guilds were called out and ordered to take over the guarding of the senate, the bank and the public buildings (it was another ancient duty or privilege), and a group of young boys whipped up the crowds into a frenzy by saying the bread was bad, and their leader waltzed around the town with a piece of it stuck on the bayonet of a gun taken off a guard outside the viceregal palace.

The soldiers dared not interfere and the field was open for revolt. The rebels took hold of arms from the port, stormed the Vicaria prison and set the prisoners free. Fogliani retired to his palace and surrounded himself with troops; the Swiss Guards came out of the Castello but retired again quickly, and the cavalry rode into the centre of the town where, of course, they were useless. The crowds were now shouting against Fogliani. Night fell and Archbishop Filangieri, who was popular with the masses, to all intents and purposes took over – he organised the parish priests and confirmed that the guilds of the artisans should continue patrolling the town. The next day, the mob, together with the guilds (now about 40,000 all told), were in complete control. They first checked that the archbishop was in charge as they had demanded, arranged cannons around the viceregal palace, got the doors open, let out the soldiers who offered no resistance and sent in a delegation to speak to Fogliani, who was hearing confession. Under threat of death, he agreed to leave through the jeering crowd: he sailed for Messina.

Archbishop Filangeri took over, greatly helped by the guilds of craftsmen who, however powerful, were undoubtedly the puppets of the barons. The ringleaders were later executed. Although subsequently the army had gently taken back control from the guilds, the political account with the craftsmen (and indirectly the barons)[28] needed more time. Fogliani lingered on as governor in Messina for some months, while the archbishop was made governor of Sicily, but by the end of 1774 Fogliani was relieved of his post.

When Marcantonio Colonna, Prince of Stigliano, was made viceroy in 1775 it must have been crystal clear in Naples that the policy of keeping the Sicilian barons sweet had failed badly, not that Stigliano did much about this. It appears that he was instructed that the barons should pay their debts like everybody else; his entourage was rather more markedly Neapolitan than was normal, his food policy was rather less protectionist and he put a few more barons in jail, but he was hardly very active, and after not many years in office he was as anxious to get away from Palermo as Caracciolo was loathe to arrive.

Part Three

Viceroy

Vivace assai

7

Settling In

꧁ꕤ꧂

The new 66-year-old viceroy finally turned up in Palermo on 14 October 1781, more than a year after his initial appointment. He was sent there by a government in Naples seeking a change of policy, a balance to Prime Minister Sambuca's influence from Naples. He was preceded by a reputation for having dangerous libertine friendships in France and he went with considerable reluctance, but also with very clear ideas about what his life's experience commanded him to do. Very soon his much-loved Parisian *bonhomie* disintegrated into apprehension, irritation and anger.

The ceremony upon his arrival was described in some detail by the diarist Marquis Villabianca.[1] Caracciolo's ship arrived in port on the evening of Sunday 14 October, but he was obliged by etiquette to stay on board until the next morning so that he could be greeted by a 'congratulatory ambassadorial group' sent out in a special felucca by the senate of Palermo. When he managed to reach the shore shortly afterwards he was met by an imposing array of officials and conducted to an interim house, where he was obliged to put up for the next three days for a grinding round of receptions and presentations, all conducted with immense pomp and circumstance. The day of his *possesso* (i.e. his official instalment) had been fixed, no doubt by the local authorities, for 17 October and on that day he was conducted in great ceremony, escorted by cavalry and other military, with flashing unsheathed swords to the Casa Professa church where, among other things, he was required to swear to uphold the privileges of the city of Palermo with gloves and those of the Kingdom of Sicily without gloves. He was then conducted to the palace where he was to reside officially as viceroy. In the evening there was a gala theatre performance. It is almost certain that, of all the things that occurred in those four days, this is the only one that he would have tolerated.

This fairly full description of his arrival has been given for two reasons, in the first place because it reveals the absolute importance of the outward demonstration of tradition for Sicilian society of the time, and secondly because it was written by the Marquis of Villabianca. The above description is in fact a short resumé of several pages in Villabianca's diary. What emerges is that the writer felt proud that these traditional ceremonies were being bestowed on the neo-viceroy. The Marquis of Villabianca is considered by many Italian historians to be the epitome of the Sicilian baronial thought at that time; he wrote 22 volumes of diaries, among many other works, and came to hate Caracciolo's reforms. It is significant that in that very first entry in his diary he describes Caracciolo thus:

> He was born of the same excellent Caracciolo family of the Princes of Avellino ... from the now dominant city of Naples, from the branch of the Dukes of Santa Teodora, being a cadet of that house, which in effect not having much financial substance, he was obliged in his home country to exercise the profession of a minor lawyer as a young man ... but on account of his talent, today one can say with the poet: He is not a Prince among us because of his ancestors, but because of his virtue and because of his merit.

That might sound like a compliment, but from Villabianca, who was a rabid aristocrat, one suspects it was not. Also significant is the reference to the fact that Naples was now the dominant city. Not only was Caracciolo not perhaps a true-blue aristocrat at heart, but he was also an outsider.

Although under no delusions about the enormity of the task facing him, the new viceroy was buoyed up by the knowledge, the absolute conviction, that the rational changes he intended to introduce must inevitably succeed not only because they were ethically right, but also because they were rationally correct and had been demonstrated to work successfully elsewhere in Europe. This conviction meant that in introducing his reforms, despite his background in diplomacy, he was completely lacking in tact – and it could be said he *dashed* at them. A certain amount of this energy was stoked by his genuine dislike of barons in general, which has been already noted, and the Sicilian barons in particular, given his Neapolitan background. His desire to strip them of their privileges and the church of its, and his wholehearted acceptance of his brief to restore the monarchy to its authority on the island, should be understood as he saw it – as a means to alleviate the poor, dismantle abuses, reform the law and the administration, introduce a proper *catasto* (land survey) so that equitable taxes could be levied, encourage trade, improve revenues for the royal exchequer and 'liquidate the inheritance of the past'.[2] His ideas were crystal clear and consistent, and had been forming quite consciously in his correspondence ever since his days in Turin, but despite the reputation that he had gained in Paris for lethargy (he and Galiani had been famous for their laziness) his first two and a half months in Palermo, practically from the day he was installed, were marked by a frenzy of administrative activity that would have left his Parisian friends quite speechless. It must be remembered that he had no experience at all in administration or government of any kind.

His first task, then, was to impose the authority of the king through his own viceregal person. A *circolare* was issued on 29 November 1781 (and confirmed on 16 December of the same year) that re-issued in no uncertain terms a royal order of 1737 requiring all representatives of tribunals, courts, ministries and other bodies – be they secular, ecclesiastical, military or political – with the right to present any sort of petition to the court or the government in Naples to do so via the viceroy. This was to stamp on the habit of wholesale rejection of the 'normal' channels when the personal interests of privileged people or institutions were involved. All representations were to be submitted to the viceroy with the seal still unfixed before being sent on to the king. To underline the point, another despatch was issued on 17 December 1781 to the president of the *Gran Corte* (Airoldi, whom we have seen at this time being described to Galiani as the barbarous pope of the Sicilian legal scene), the court that had surreptitiously taken over charge of censorship from the viceroys: the despatch allowed the court to continue publishing all printed papers, edicts, prints, bands and so on, but only after the viceroy had seen and approved a copy.

Caracciolo's next move concerned the army, with which his predecessors had played a very deferential role. From the very first he made it clear that he, as viceroy, was the military as well as political chief on the island, and this not only for reasons of re-establishment of monarchical authority, but also because the army was not well controlled and therefore a source of social disruption. The commander-in-chief was summoned and informed that the viceroy enjoyed all jurisdiction and authority in both political and military spheres, that the king's orders were to be transmitted via the viceroy to the commander, and that the latter had to use the viceroy to communicate with the secretary for war: '[F]urthermore the Viceroy himself could give orders to all the commanders and military units in the Kingdom', as the wording of the final despatch has it.[3]

In the meantime, the fearful problem of the price of bread had again reared its head. On 20 November 1781 there were threats of public uprisings and surprisingly, in Villabianca's words,

> A great deal was achieved to quieten down these public resentments by the repeated visits made by the new Viceroy to the public ovens and market squares, denouncing those responsible for producing bad bread and threatening them with personal and pecuniary punishment.[4]

It must have been quite clear by this time that the new viceroy was no *passalettere* – the eminent figurehead that just shuffled papers around in the intervals between receptions – which the barons had been used to up to Caracciolo's arrival. The inevitable reactions were soon to be heard.

In a society where appearances were everything, Caracciolo took pleasure in making it clear that he was not on the side of the Establishment. When, for instance, he appeared solemnly for the first time in public at the cathedral in Palermo during a pontifical mass, sitting on a throne representing the papal legacy conferred on the Sicilian kings by Urban II in 1098, he pointedly did not cover his head when the priest offered incense. The scandal was enormous because this act flouted the traditional prerogatives of the Sicilian kings.[5] In the same spirit, he insisted on reading himself the opening speech of the first *Parlamento* in 1782, rather than leave this to the *Protonotaro*, as tradition required.[6] And to be quite sure everybody understood his position, when the time came to be formally sworn in for his second term of office in 1784, instead of being embroiled in the usual complicated ceremonial rigmarole, which everyone looked forward to, he arrived unaccompanied and informally attired at the cathedral in a hired coach.[7] He also frequented the singer Marina Balducci, whom he had known in Paris, which was noted with some distress by Palermo society. He wrote of her to Galiani that

> Only Balducci seems to be a female of the species of which I am a male. On the other hand one must play with these cards because I value the society of women as a hedge against too intimate a society with men, who are here too intent either *à tirer le vers du nez* or in distorting the things one says.[8]

While on the island she was entertained at Caracciolo's table and receptions in an atmosphere of joking and great informality, wholly at odds with what most (though perhaps not everybody) in prevailing society thought fit. Villabianca stuck into his diary a four-sided printed pamphlet containing a heartfelt cry of despair in very poor verse at the departure of Marina Balducci by Signor Giuseppe Gazzaniga, the celebrated Veronese *Maestro di Capella*.[9]

In his first recorded letter to Minister Acton in Naples, on 12 June 1782, Caracciolo talks of 'complaints and accusations against me', which had been conveyed secretly to the king, concerning

> omissions during ecclesiastical functions and the occasional imprudence in my private life, nothing at all that has anything to do with the public good, equity, justice, honour, and above all service to the King ... There are three methods that the Sicilians use to frighten those that govern them ... the first is the fear of the people, the second is the fear of satire, the third is accusations to the King concerning customs and religion. The first two have not been successful against me; they have therefore had recourse to attack me personally, but they are mistaken because I am inflexible: they can break me but never bend me.[10]

Meanwhile, the viceroy was moving ahead on other fronts. One of the first things he did was issue a despatch (18 December 1781) to the *Capitano di Giustizia*, the Marquis di Santa Croce, ordering him to choose 60 lawyers, 'that is to say fifteen from each part of the city, so that one of them every night should take a commanding role in the night rounds', for the greater public peace (the current ones were corrupt, and recognised as such). On the face of it, this would seem a rather harmless, idealistic act, but there were various complicated aspects concerning it. First of all the night round, or *'Rondo'*, was the prerogative of the craftsmen's guilds and as such needed attention and, eventually, reform, given the role they had played in the riots that had led to the overthrow of Viceroy Fogliani in 1773. Secondly, the lawyers were a privileged class. In Villabianca's words, they were

> extremely respectable, destined for the service and command
> of the republic in the affairs of State and of prime importance,
> and not less privileged and worthy than persons of noble and
> feudal families.[11]

The Spanish had had the lawyers excused from all public duties and they were furious at having this lowly job thrust on them, and at night no less. They immediately set about protesting, and the next year, as early as February, the lawyers were released from their unpleasant new duty. Caracciolo also asked the *Giunta dei Presidenti e Consultori*, in November 1781, to study 'the ways by which a public burial ground may be opened, where bodies may better be taken care of and the air is not contaminated by the smell'. Again, this directive may seem harmless and idealistic, but burial was a problem, as nobody wanted to be interred outside a church, and Caracciolo had to fight hard for his new cemetery, as we shall see later. The same *Giunta* was asked to consider 'if it is possible to establish in the capital and in nearby towns a public market for all types of foodstuffs, in what days of the week and with what privileges and exemptions' (23 and 25 November 1781).[12] On 7 November 1781 Caracciolo sent a despatch to the *Deputazione delle Strade*, the body that was supposed to look after the roads, saying that he was displeased 'that so far the 1752 plan for paving the main streets of this capital has not been executed', for which reason 'not only is it not convenient for the citizens but neither is it for the salubrity of the air', and enjoined the deputation 'to examine as soon as possible the projects already made, and propose others if it considers them more expedient and easier'. However, nobody seemed to be moving fast enough, because on 31 December 1781 Caracciolo ordered the poor *Deputazione delle Strade* to get on with paving the main streets of Palermo, as set out in the original 1752 plan, as well as urging the implementation of a 1778 parliamentary resolution for the building of provincial roads. He had also ordered the magistrate in charge of commerce (decree of 18 December 1781) to issue bands inviting commercial ships to gather in the port of Trapani at the end of February and the beginning of March, where 'they will be received under the escort of royal ships of war' in convoy to be protected from the attacks of the North African corsairs, who were a very real threat.

While all this was going on, Caracciolo had the time to ban the exaction by the parishes of all funeral dues (7 November 1781) and to abolish the fixed price and weight of bread (13 November 1781), both these measures being designed to help the poor, and to issue a curiously uncharacteristic despatch on 26 December 1781 to the citizens of Palermo urging them to display a greater sense of seriousness in life, prohibiting them, in fact, masques in the coming carnival season, the use of which 'offends the public decorum and the respect due to the Magistrature'.

Ecclesiastical reforms were not as strenuous as might have been expected, perhaps because the church was less involved in Sicilian politics than it had been on the mainland. Caracciolo revised the statutes of the confraternities in some detail (even to the extent of the standards they bore in processions), reformed some of them and dissolved others (devolving their patrimonies either to charities or to the new cemetery); he organised clerical alms collections and marriage provisions on sound bases; severe limits were laid down against excesses in the initiation rites for monks and nuns (the numbers of cakes and candles etc.); he suppressed various White Benedictine convents and had monastic chapter affairs subjected to viceregal visits. He also tried to prevent church authorities on the island communicating with their superiors elsewhere, complained to the Archbishop of Palermo that his clergy were lazy and frivolous, and encouraged them to open schools in their cloisters. Caracciolo also tried to curb the right of asylum and to interfere with the ecclesiastical courts.[13] Early on he had decreed that bishops should be disallowed from citing people in a court of law, let alone imprisoning them without producing documentary evidence for viceregal inspection and approval and the guarantee of a defence lawyer,[14] and later on he was to abolish the *Parlamento*'s Ecclesiastical chamber's right to ask the pope's permission for voting new taxes.[15]

On the purely moral front he was equally active in his reforms, and he began straight away. The ban against the use of indecent masques in the carnival season has already been mentioned – this was issued at the end of 1781. From that time onwards, at various stages of his administration provisions were taken against the following malpractices[16]: betting; anonymous letters and denouncements; inflammatory or alarming notices; the explosion of firecrackers or other fireworks against private houses; the use of drums at night; certain dangerous popular sports, such as the running of cows and heifers to resemble the Spanish *corrida*; excessively luxurious funerals; prostitutes; criminals and the frequency of certain crimes; urban rubbish;

the slaking of linen within domestic walls; vaccination; burials in churches and, where not possible, the obligation to build communal cemeteries; provisions in favour of prisons; hospitals and houses of redemption for lost women and houses of correction for wayward boys; schools, which he wanted to institute in every corner of the island.

Caracciolo's attention was, given his background, very much concerned with legal matters right from the start. In a series of early despatches he tackled head on the continuous clashes that existed between the various jurisdictions and the artificial procedural delays that proliferated, both of which resulted in his office being submerged with appeals. He defined the jurisdictional boundaries better and rescued from oblivion certain opportune norms, which he imposed with rigour; he abolished certain privileged courts; he deprived the president of the *Gran Corte Criminale e Civile* of certain attributes he had usurped from the viceregal office, and stamped on other autonomous claims that this magistrate was making *vis à vis* the viceroy.[17] He ordered – presumably it was necessary – the *avvocato fiscale* of the *Gran Corte* to make sure that the order for the liberation of prisoners was actually carried out once their term had been served (6 December 1781). In terms of local justice, he formally warned the *giurati* (locally elected magistrates) of both the baronial and demesnial towns against interfering in any way with the administration of civil or criminal justice, which was the legal competence of the *capitanali* courts, and threatened them with punishments if they strayed from their own jurisdiction, which was limited to food supply.[18]

Narrowing his aim a little, he began the battle against the barons. On 28 December 1781 he issued a series of injunctions that hit closer to this particular mark. The first was an indirect attack, as it affected daughters: it recalled a *circolare* that the *Gran Corte* had promulgated in 1775, requiring a 'reform in the useless expenditure that one is wont to make when young girls put on the nuns habit' and spelled out a simpler and much less luxurious ceremony. This would certainly have annoyed many a noble family, some of whose daughters would be destined for the convent, and all of whom were interested in ceremony. Less ceremonial, however, was the injunction that the barons were not to deny their vassals their liberty or the cultivation of land outside their territory until they had finished cultivating their lord's, requiring them furthermore to honour exactly the laws of the kingdom that conceded greater liberty to the peasants.[19] And on 29 December 1781 he issued a despatch for the punishment of

> anyone connected with the Tribunal of the Sant'Ufizio [the Inquisition] found carrying a carbine and any other sort of arms without the authorisation of the *Gran Corte*, unless he is carrying out his duties for the said Tribunal.

This was the beginning of Caracciolo's attack on the Inquisition, but it must be noted that the main reason for this was not so much that the Inquisition was a threat to society, but that it was a *shame* on society, and had to go for this reason, as well as – and more importantly – the fact that it was a hotbed of baronial privilege.

This flurry of reform, this stirring up of things, did not go down at all well. Sicily had not seen two and a half months like this for centuries. Although it had been known that Caracciolo had been the friend of dangerous people in France, the Sicilians had been prepared to give him the benefit of the doubt at the beginning. Even Villabianca in the early days was not against him, but the diarist's tone was changing: '[T]he customs honoured by Sicily were very different from those of France, among which the Viceroy had lived'[20] he wrote at the time, and from this point on he voiced the outrage of the barons at the atrocities that Caracciolo was to attempt on Sicily.

As Caracciolo wrote in the first surviving letter to his minister of referral in Naples, Sir John Acton, the minister of marine affairs, on 12 June 1782:

> My zeal for the reform of abuses, for the observance of the laws and for some newly established institution or that evidently needs to be established are Caracciolo's offence; these are my true crimes; the government of Prince Corsini [Viceroy 1737–47] was liked by the Sicilians, because he limited himself to a simple *passalettere*, a shuffler of letters. That is how the Sicilians want their Viceroys.[21]

It has already been mentioned that Caracciolo came to Sicily with absolutely no experience in government and it must be added that there was no semblance of a reform party on the island as there was, to some extent, on the mainland, so he was intellectually and physically isolated. He therefore relied very heavily on his two professional advisors, neither of whom was Sicilian. His secretary was the Neapolitan Giuseppe Gargano, a shy, hard-working, honest man of wide views, but not those to be expected in one so close to the centre of radical reforms. His top legal advisor, the *consultore*, Saverio Simonetti, though born in Calabria, had been educated in Naples. His was a first-rate legal brain able to cut through the thick undergrowth of Sicilian legal vegetation and reduce it to order from the point of view of the monarchy and the treasury. Simonetti was also rigid, severe and somewhat pedantic, but both he and Gargano were seen as 'Neapolitan', which was much worse. Caracciolo himself also erred very decidedly on the side of authoritarianism, even if, as in everything, there was a theoretical reason for doing so. As he wrote to Acton:

> This craze for committees in our times is well known; it is also a certainty that ... a great work can never be born of a

committee, that is to say of many heads, because the great and the sublime work is formed by a single mould and not of separate bits and pieces stuck together later ... And if then committees have the advantage that no single person has authority in them, they have the equal disadvantage that nobody is responsible for any bad that results.[22]

This is a pupil of Tanucci talking about Enlightened despotism, but Tanucci's time was over. Not only that: what Caracciolo never fully understood was that, theoretically speaking, even if he had had the king's undying backing, he could never legally have been a despot in Sicily because he was only the king's minister, and, anyway, subject to that kingdom's constitution, as was the king himself.[23] It was not surprising that baronial backs rose the moment Caracciolo put pen to paper – phrases such as 'subversive innovations', 'abuse of power and harshness of government' and 'absolute power and tyranny' abound in the archives of the time,[24] the diaries of Villabianca record the horror of conservative Sicily at his every move, and even the less-privileged classes were put out by some of Caracciolo's moves, moves such as banning masques in carnival, not to mention other later even less subtly thought-out measures.

Tact was not one of Caracciolo's virtues. Nor did he help himself as time went on by insisting on governing the island through just Simonetti, his *consultore*, and Gargano, his secretary, whom the Sicilians mistrusted: Neapolitans were apparently flouting the Sicilian constitution, and he himself limited his contact with the king through Acton, whom the king did not particularly like.

8

The Abolition of the Inquisition

Quite unsurprisingly, this most unexpected flurry of vexatious activity by the newly arrived viceroy stirred up a chorus of protests from all sides. Among the first and loudest came from the body of lawyers (which included, incidentally, judges from the *Gran Corte* and the *Consistorio*), who were in uproar that they had been demeaned by being ordered to be nightwatchmen by Caracciolo. Their protest went straight to Naples. In the words of the diarist Villabianca:

> There were advanced by this class the most insistent appeal and complaint to the Government and the matter was put before the *Giunta Suprema de' Presidenti e Consultore*. The advocate Bernardino Denti presented an excellent document in their defence, laden with erudite arguments from Roman history and also from the history of the Sicilian Nation, as well as pertinacious facts concerning the case. Numerous royal documents and privileges were thoroughly studied and shown to the consulting Ministers so that they should be aware of the dignity and decorum of these laureates.[1]

Nobody doubted the outcome, which was in fact announced in the lawyers' favour in February. This small example of opposition was emblematic of many others. When reform is in the air, vigorous class actions sprout up to protect traditional privileges and to block change of any sort.

The lawyers were not the only protesters, of course. After the banning of the funeral tax and the parish priests' asking for contributions from the poor, the priests protested directly to the senate of Palermo and many petitions were sent to the king from all parts of the island on the grounds that the priests' livelihoods were being put in jeopardy.[2] Nor was the Army of Christ the only army up in arms: the commander in chief was already writing that the viceroy may have a military position as captain general of the province and could impart orders to the army, but these concerned the political objectives of the government, and should be directed to the commander-in-chief and not his subordinates.[3] For the moment the controversy simmered sourly and without solution: it was not until 30 March 1783 that the struggle was resolved in a compromise (the commander was given military supremacy, while the viceroy retained the political control).

The barons expressed their violent disagreement in active gossip, much of which is reflected in the pages of Villabianca's diaries, and the situation was not helped by Caracciolo's apparent feelings of superiority where they were concerned – a far cry from Fogliani's policy of wining and dining them. Gossip began to creep into print and a particularly unpleasant piece of satire against Caracciolo was deemed by him to have issued from the house of the Marquis of Geraci, a most haughty family with whom the viceroy was not destined to get on at all well. It must be said that Caracciolo did not show much eighteenth-century love of reason or toleration in his reaction to this campaign. While he felt attacked in his honour by a despicable baronial class, it must also be explained that he had an enormous respect for the power of the written word and he chose also to see satire as a danger to the state as a whole; he even wrote to the Marquis of Sambuca, the principal minister in Naples:

because such libels could cause various and considerable inconveniences, even the death of people at the hands of the individuals the satires accuse them of offending, and from this even give rise to some popular unrest, unless a stop is put to it, with all due exemplary punishment, unless all access is closed in the future to the issuing of similar sarcastic writings.[4]

This seems strange, but it was an entirely political reaction on Caracciolo's part, because his later actions were wholeheartedly against any form of censure, but he acted vigorously to hunt down the authors, offering a reward of 300 ounces and a free pardon to anybody revealing the name of the author of this particular attack. As a result of much activity he had three young gentlemen arrested – Giuseppe Valguarnera, Gaspare Palermo and Vincenzo Ugo – but the result was to nobody's satisfaction, as the court ruled that they were to apologise *politically* to the viceroy and ask for his pardon *personally*. This great respect for the power of the written word led Caracciolo to extremes. Villabianca probably put it best when he wrote 'In substance it was a lot of noise about a childish prank which it would have been better to pass over,'[5] but he had a blind spot about being attacked in print, both as a person and as a representative of the king.

This quite violent reaction to opposition in print was not just a personal quirk; it also applied when Caracciolo deemed literature damaging to the legitimate interests of the state. In 1783, for example, he had the works of two long-defunct legal apologists of feudal rights, Pietro de Gregorio and Francesco Milanese, publicly burnt by the hangman. The two books, *De judiciis causarum feudalium* and *De concessione feudi*, were not only burnt, but stern sentences were announced for anyone who made use of them or divulged their specious theories.[6] Later on he had a similar sort of reaction, in this case to busts rather than books, when he ordered the statues of Mongitore and di Napoli, that symbol of baronial legal revolt to royal authority in feudal matters, together with two unknowns, Cascini and Casimiro Drago, to be removed from the senate in Palermo. When his orders were not carried out promptly he had the police sent in at night to take the busts down and put away in a storehouse.[7] While this has its silly side, it does reflect Caracciolo's eighteenth-century conviction that ideas were real and important factors in government.

If his reactions to perceived threats from ideas were occasionally extreme, there were also occasions when his measures to counter practical challenges to viceregal authority were of an exceptionally radical nature as well. In a letter to Acton at this time (27 June 1782) he wrote, for instance:

> Your Excellency would not believe how easy it is to put order into Sicily[;] I was surprised, one can make a good job of it much more easily than with the Kingdom of Naples; there are two or three grand operations that seem difficult, and would be very easy to carry out. One, for example, would be for the Viceroy and the Tribunals and the whole shop should pack up and go off for three years to Messina. Oh! What a fount this would be of great things! I should like just for a moment to be transported there [Naples] to talk to the *Padroni* [the king and queen] and Your Excellency and would like to make you 'touch with your hands' how easy it is to put a sword to the root of all the abuses, and make this Kingdom capable of rendering up to the Exchequer another million scudi.

He added, however, that he needed the backing of Naples to do this.[8] Caracciolo's proposal to remove Sicily's capital from Palermo to Messina might seem a little far fetched, but it was a serious one. It never came to anything, though, because of the jealousies involved, the decayed state of the economy of Messina and, above all, the terrible earthquake that hit the city in February 1783. However, Caracciolo had been in contact with the governor of the city in October 1782, informing him that he intended to transfer the capital there in the spring of 1783.[9] Whether or not he would have been allowed to do so is open to speculation, as the king was often to let him down when his assistance was most needed, but the determination was there. It is worth noting that one of the main arguments for moving the capital to Messina was that the Royal Exchequer would have been better served.

Caracciolo is mostly remembered today as the man who abolished the Inquisition. It is true that he was responsible for terminating 'the terrible monster', as he himself described it in a letter to his friend D'Alembert, but it is also true that this body was no longer much of a monster and far from what it had once been when he ended its already feeble existence. By this time the Inquisition was no longer the defender of the Catholic faith against Moors, Jews and Protestants, using the worst kinds of torture, and not even a secret spy ring of supreme cunning. It was, however, a social force and a legal association with a tribunal and vast untaxed patrimony that had been accumulated as a result of condemnations and bequests, which had acquired many noble associates.

The fact is, though, that the decision to abolish the Inquisition could not have been Caracciolo's alone: it had to come from the king through his prime minister, Sambuca, which is exactly what happened. The general background was prepared by Empress Maria Theresa, with a policy of not filling vacancies in the Institution's structure when they occurred in her Italian territories. The legal background was prepared by Simonetti (who had been Viceroy Stigliano's *consultore* before Caracciolo). However, among Caracciolo's first acts on arriving, as we have already seen, was the forbidding of members of the Tribunal of the Inquisition from carrying arms unless on official business.

For some time it had been widely felt that the government was considering moving against the Inquisition, since the posts of two provincial inquisitors had already been vacant for two years and it was not unduly surprising that, on 9 February 1782, Grand Inquisitor Monsignor Ventimiglia protested concerning the matter of these two vacant provincial posts: '[I]f it was the tacit desire to annul the *Sant'Uffizio* [the Inquisition], it might be better to declare it abolished outright.'[10] On 22 January 1782 the viceroy took further steps against the Institution by suspending its right to print edicts and excommunications during Lent and twice again in February, on the basis that such actions could disturb the minds of ignorant people and produce scandal, a decision that was forthwith upheld by the king.[11] The fact that the king was with Caracciolo gave him courage, if he needed it. He decided to abolish the whole Inquisition there and then, probably realising that this was expected of him and that his authority would be bolstered by a quick, clean result, but also that this would be a symbolic gain for liberty and exactly what the century required of him.

On 13 March 1782, without royal instructions from Naples, he ordered the *consultore*, Saverio Simonetti, to go to the Inquisition's headquarters, the *Palazzo Steri*, and 'take into your care all and every writing that pertains to the Inquisition and especially books and registers of income',[12] which effectively brought the institution to a close. At the time he found only three aged prisoners in the cells, one an old woman who had absolutely no desire to be liberated because she was incapable of looking after herself. All the other prisoners had apparently been secretly freed before Simonetti's arrival and, since this was deemed most incorrect, Grand Inquisitor Ventimiglia was firmly reprimanded. The formal closure came a little later, on 27 March, when, in the presence of the viceroy, his secretary Giuseppe Gargano read out to the Archbishop of Palermo and representatives of all the main Sicilian magistratures the royal decree suppressing the Inquisition and the infamous three iron cages containing human remains for the edification of the public were destroyed. Simonetti made a careful inventory of the patrimony, which was liquidated in favour of the treasury, most of the proceeds going to charity, and most of the needy ex-dependents were adequately pensioned off.

A far more delicate question was what to do with the archives, manuscripts and books that had been accumulated over the centuries by the Inquisition. Among other things, these documents contained mountains of secrets concerning generations of leading families, a fact that made many powerful figures apprehensive of what might happen to them. There was also the intrinsic historical and literary value of many of these documents, which actively concerned a small but growing group of intellectuals much favoured by the viceroy. Caracciolo had them all sealed, but was for donating them to public libraries or shipping them to Naples. Naturally, the *Giunta* in Palermo refused point blank to do anything of the kind.

As early as 23 March 1782 the priest in charge of the *Real Pubblica Libreria del Senato*, Angelini by name, had petitioned Caracciolo to the effect that he had heard it was the king's intention to abolish the Inquisition and, if that were the case, could all the books in the Institution's possession be made available to the *Real Libreria del Senato*, where they would find a safe haven and could be consulted by literary people during their researches. Caracciolo, evidently in favour of a move of this sort, forwarded the petition to the king. A reply from Naples arrived in February of the following year, before the viceroy had effectively closed the Inquisition; it gave the royal consent to the petition, but required Caracciolo to appoint two scholars of proven honesty to analyse the material, to select those works that were suitable for a public library and to seal the rest up. He did this (one of the two scholars, Canon Barbarici, incidentally, was a close collaborator of Simonetti's), and, despite considerable high-level bureaucratic obstructionism, a large number of books and documents were saved and shelved in the *Real Libreria del Senato* before the rest were destroyed.[13] That was, in fact, as far Caracciolo could manage to go against establishment, bureaucracy and the absolute desire for secrecy in high places. So, finally, on 27 July 1783, with the viceroy participating in person, the rest of the books and documents were, together with vestments, instruments of torture and even some unpleasant paintings, piled on to a bonfire. The blaze lasted for more than 24 hours.

Villabianca's reaction to the initial announcement of abolition was unsurprising: 'It was an event which filled the whole country with novelty and stupor',[14] he wrote, but when the occupation took place some days later[15] he was one of the party and seemed less surprised, though he accused Caracciolo of indulging his usual 'Neapolitan childishness' when he threw a Spanish picture, together with all the yellow vestments worn by the heretics under Inquisition, as well as the hats and various instruments used by soothsayers, magicians, witches and bigamists, on to the fire.

Caracciolo, on the other hand, was filled with pride and wrote to D'Alembert in Paris a letter that, though edited of polite references to the unimportance of the event,[16] was subsequently printed in the French newspaper *Mercure de France*:

> To tell you the truth, my dear friend, I felt very touched and I cried: it is the one and only time I have been moved to thank Heaven to have removed me from Paris to serve as an instrument in this great work.[17]

Although this was not in reality a complicated victory, it was considered a great one, a definitive break with the past, and

D'Alembert was probably right to edit his friend's genuine letter and present it to the public as advertising a European event. To the *philosophe* in Paris, the fall of the Inquisition was a blow to the Middle Ages' mind-set and a victory for Reason. It was without doubt seen as a great event in Sicily at the time. It should, incidentally, be noted that although the church was not upset by the abolition of the Inquisition, the barons certainly were, because with it disappeared many of their attendant privileges.

The patrimony of the Inquisition[18] was appropriated by the crown, but provision was made for life pensions for the principal ex-officials. Most of the money was dedicated to charitable ends, some even found its way to the '*Casa di Nostra Signora delle Derelitte*,'[19] an organisation that looked after redeemed prostitutes, but a considerable amount of it was invested by Caracciolo in the *Academia*, the basis of the future University of Palermo, an institution very close to his heart. Inquisition money was instrumental for the foundation of the botanical garden, a chemical laboratory, an anatomical theatre, a museum of natural sciences and an astronomical observatory.[20] Caracciolo had Giuseppe Piazza put in charge of the observatory and he presumably would have appreciated the irony of the Inquisitional funds when, much later, in 1801, he discovered the first ever asteroid, Ceres. The *Regia Accademia degli Studi di Palermo* had originally been set up with money from the dissolution of the Jesuits in 1779, but Caracciolo quickly gave it his attention, and made it into an active centre for study, particularly in physics, law, mathematics, chemistry and natural science. By 1784 it had opened its doors to 1,600 students.

9

Clearing the Decks

❧❧❧

y far the greatest battle of Caracciolo's viceregency was the one
he engaged in to establish a just method of assessing and
collecting taxes in Sicily. He fought with all his strength, against
fierce opposition from the barons and a lack of the king's backing,
to carry out a land survey, a *catasto*, so that the assessment could
be based on reality. This was an idea that he brought with him to
the island – we have already seen that he was urging the
Piedmontese catastal system on Tanucci as well as Maria Theresa's
catasto in Milan from the time he went to Turin, and the basic idea
can be traced back to the teachings of his old master Genovesi.[1]

In Sicily he began the long and arduous process later on in
1782 when the General *Parlamento* met in April, but the struggle
with the Sicilian *Parlamento*, the barons, all the vested interests
and, in the last analysis, the Bourbon monarchy itself was a very
long affair that lasted beyond his tenure of office. Meanwhile,
before, during and after this struggle, which was by far the closest
to his heart, there was a whole series of other reforms to be dealt
with, all of them concerned with social justice, as Caracciolo saw
it – lowering the haughty, raising the downtrodden, ironing out
twisted legislation and cleaning up corroded administration.

One of his earliest acts on arrival heralded his attentions
as far as previous administrations were concerned. On 23
February 1781 he issued an injunction to the Protonotary to the

effect that for the election of every sort of official in the future there should be a choice of three candidate names instead of the usual solitary one for the nomination and election of any vacancy.[2] This struck a sharp blow in favour of widening the choice of officials, selecting perhaps the better man and limiting the facility of the powerful to place their people willy-nilly where they wished, a facility that had remained undisturbed for time immemorial. On 4 June 1782 he felt he had to remind the members of the senate of Palermo and its subsidiary officers that they did not hold their positions for life, but only *pro tempore*.[3] Caracciolo also publicly reprimanded the advocate fiscal of the *Gran Corte* for issuing a two-month safe conduct to a military gentleman, requiring him to submit a written justification,[4] and re-affirmed in a minute to Acton on 11 July 1783 that no tribunal, magistrate, court or minister could use the king's name without the viceroy's permission.[5]

These might seem paltry matters, but they were not at all: the clarification to the senate and the reprimand to the judge were of consequence to the society of the time and it was necessary that the government of Naples was behind Caracciolo in what he was doing. His correspondence with Acton in August and September 1783 was much taken up with the case of a certain Dolce, a public official who had defaulted to the tune of 17,000 ounces, but might be reinstated with the help of important friends, while the king was left with the debt. It was essential, believed Caracciolo, to urge the king to establish an irrevocable norm whereby whoever nominated cashiers, treasurers or other officials that dealt with public money should be financially answerable for eventual shortcomings.[6] His repeated pleas for a measure of this sort were not, however, to be answered until 31 January 1783, when strict regulations were finally issued by Naples.

A major step was taken on the jurisdictional front on 1 August 1782 when Caracciolo ordered that all judges and magistrates, captains and other officials (whether state or baronial) be subject to the *sindacatura* (an ancient custom of the Kingdom of Sicily whereby all members of the public had the right to complain before a superior judge about supposed injustice suffered at their hands at the end of their term of office), which, incidentally, was confirmed as *annual*. Quite obviously, Caracciolo was very enthusiastic about this measure, but quite unsurprisingly he was very much in the minority and had great difficulty in implementing it. Royal confirmation of this reform (and another that allowed peasants to cultivate lands other than their lords' before their lords' harvest) was received by Caracciolo with great satisfaction. In a letter to Acton 17 February 1783 he wrote not only that

> they will restore liberty to the unfortunate subjects of the King, oppressed or slaves, and will destroy the power and credit of the Barons in their feudal lands ... [but, more interestingly] ... the inconstant changeability that often occurs in the Royal determination makes me tremble, and I assure Your Excellency that, despite the confirmation of the two Circulars, written in Naples, they flatter themselves that they will have them withdrawn. Your Excellency cannot imagine the harm that comes from frequent changes in principles, ideas and dispositions, be they legal or economic, to Good Government, and from which a certain sense of ridicule derives that gives birth to two sorts of sentiments in the population: one a contempt for those who govern and the other an sense of audacity for daring souls to take over the situation.[7]

This lack of royal confidence in support for his reforms in Naples remained with Caracciolo during his time in Sicily, and it was often justified. At about this time he had an unsuccessful brush with the aristocratic religious congregation, the *Compagnia dei Bianchi*. He attacked them from the point of view of the administration of justice and came up against privileges that were too much for him.

The facts were these. A certain Alicia Aprile, who had murdered her niece and appropriated her possessions, had been condemned to death; the *Compagnia dei Bianchi*, however, had the privilege of pardoning a condemned criminal once a year, on Good Friday, and the president, in the person of the Marquis of Spaccaforno, chose to pardon Alicia Aprile. Caracciolo denied the privilege; Spaccaforno insisted. The matter went to the *Corte dei Presidenti e Consulente* and then to the supreme council of state of the *Real Corte* in Naples; the *Compagnia* won its case and had its privileges confirmed, much to the satisfaction of the barons, which was faithfully registered in the diary of Villabianca. Caracciolo did need his victories and his help from Naples – his authority suffered when they were lacking.

He was at work on the commercial front as well. In general terms his plan was to open up the island by simplifying administration and excise duties, building roads, establishing general markets, restoring liberties to agriculture and eliminating piracy. On this last point, as we have already seen, he had been at work from the start, arranging a convoy system in the port of Trapani. In the early months of 1783 he was again preoccupied with the problem of the North African corsairs, imploring, for instance, in a 23 May 1785 minute to Acton for 'opportune orders so that royal warships should never distance themselves from the seas of Sicily in these very dangerous times'.[8]

His market plans went ahead and the general market in Palermo was officially opened on 1 July 1782 with the general cattle market following four days later, due notice having been given to officials all over the island in good time to allow all buyers and sellers access without any sort of hindrance. Nor was anybody to be forced to pay duties – all were allowed to travel freely. There were great expectations, even from opponents who realised what Caracciolo was trying to do, but the result was a great failure. Villabianca describes how there were 'very few' people on the first day of the general market and at the cattle market only 'two horses and an unbroken carriage mule'; by the second day it was all over. The reason, as has already been mentioned, was that no reduction in excise duties at the actual marketplace was allowed for, so a good idea enabled to work. People may have been free to come, but had no particular incentive to do so.

Caracciolo took the earliest opportunity to make a start on what was for him the really fundamental problem, the one nearest his heart and from which his idea of justice would flow – the reform of the *catasto*. The opportunity came with the convening of the three-yearly General *Parlamento* on 30 April 1782, but this was preceded by various moves, firstly, the prohibition of the ecclesiastical branch's habit of asking permission of the pope to vote *donativi*, which has already been mentioned, on the grounds that it prejudiced the authority of the king, who owed allegiance to God alone in his own domain. This despatch of Caracciolo's, dated 23 March 1782, was backed up by a *Consulta*, a reasoned document by Simonetti, which set out the argument and stated the case that non-payment of taxes was against the teachings of Christ. It was at this point that Caracciolo suggested that *Parlamento* be called a 'congress' and the *donativo* (gift) a 'contribution'. Again, these were not considered either by Caracciolo or by his opponents as paltry matters of form, but important matters of substance. More important still was Simonetti's *Consulta* of 9 April 1782 in which Caracciolo's plans for fiscal reform were spelled out for Naples. This was a tightly argued document that had as its thesis that Sicily was potentially richer than Naples but delivered less to the treasury because 'the distribution between all those who pay is not calculated as it should be, but it is erroneous, oppressive and unjust.'

A profound analysis of the system was carried out with the spotlight particularly on the hardship of the demesnial townships and the exemption of the ecclesiastics, the errors of the last census, the iniquity of the equal division between demesnial and baronial townships, showing that the latter were three times more numerous than the former, and so on.[9]

Such were the preparations for the *Parlamento* that convened on 30 April 1782 to an opening speech read not, as convention would have it, by the *Protonotaro del Regno*, but by the viceroy himself, and in a tone that astounded many of his audience for its novelty.

> The population of Sicily has increased in certain areas, in others it has gone down; I have observed this by practical examination in many parts of the Kingdom. Furthermore, after the last census in 1747 there must even be a notable difference in the estimate of the number of estates from that date to today; wherefore I exhort this General Parlamento to ask for a new census of souls and a new valuation of lands, so that the tax burdens can be reasonably divided and so that the weakness of certain communities does not suffer from a weight, the greater part of which other wealthier and more populous communities ought to be carrying.[10]

Caracciolo did not, of course, convince the barons or the ecclesiastics, who were outraged at the content and tone of the speech, but some of the members of the Demesnial chamber did ask that the new census should be made and the request was forwarded to the king, despite the apparent dissent of the other two chambers. There was, however, open war between barons and Caracciolo at this point, with no holds barred, and the king's support became even more essential to the viceroy. A decision on the *catasto* became The Decision – everything was secondary to it, and it was anxiously awaited.

Villabianca's position was, not unexpectedly, decidedly hostile:[11]

[T]he present Viceroy of Sicily Marquis di Villamaina Domenico Caracciolo, since he is a declared enemy of the country for the ruinous way he has conducted his government so far, attempted to deprive the kingdom of Sicily of her greatest privilege, that is to say the dignity and liberty that the Sicilian nation has of being able to assemble in parliament, in a face to face dialogue with the King and meeting his needs with what money it is willing to supply.

Villabianca felt certain his peers thought as he did, as, he was sure, did the king.

While waiting for The Decision there were other things to do – paving the streets of Palermo, for example. The theory was that by paving the streets the way would be made easier for carriages; therefore, they should be made to pay a carriage tax, which was instituted. It has been suggested that there were 784 carriages circulating in Palermo at the time,[12] clearly belonging to the baronial class, but the owners did not appreciate the new tax at all. Indeed, many of them refused to pay. There were public skirmishes in the streets between the gentlemen owners and the officers of the law and many incidents of seizure for non-payment of the tax, which gave rise street scenes. The most famous of these concerned the Marchioness di Geraci, who publicly refused to pay her fine, upon which Caracciolo intervened almost personally, seized her carriage and had it auctioned in a public square. Great was the scandal and the complaints flying to Naples were as numerous as starlings. But on 21 March 1782 the main streets of Palermo began to be paved in marble (not a luxury, incidentally, because marble is a local stone) and on 3 August 1782 Caracciolo published a proclamation summarising the norms and duties for maintaining the cleanliness of the city of Palermo, including severe fines for offenders.

Still on the question of roads, but on a wider plane, the viceroy turned his attention to the construction of provincial roads, the lack of which were a serious constraint to the development of commerce and government. His plan was to build three principal roads from Palermo, one to Agrigento and Licata, one to Castellamare and Sciacca and one to Messina. The first two aroused a certain amount of interest in the barons because they facilitated the transport of corn from their estates to the port granaries, the *caricatori*, at those sea towns, but the road to Messina held no interest for them and, as a result, they interrupted the work on the whole road system.[13] Caracciolo himself saw the road to Messina as a strategic link to Naples of vital interest in the event of war, and branch roads from all three main roads an essential part of his plan to open up the island to commerce, administration and ideas.

> The King then has built the Calabrian Road to bring Sicily nearer, and the Sicilians refuse to want to be made nearer to the Kingdom of Naples? And if, in the case of war, we are not masters of the sea?[14]

His letters to Acton in August 1782 urgently requested the king's backing of the road-building scheme, emphasising the strategic, commercial, fiscal and political gains to be gained from going ahead with the plans, particularly with the Messina road. Messina was particularly important for Caracciolo, as we shall see presently. Ingrown conservatism and apparent lack of funds, however, meant that practically nothing came of all this pressure.

Privileges, baronial arrogance and the right to carry arms absorbed the viceroy's considerable energies next. In the first instance, the privileges were the responsibility of King Alfonso, who in 1448 had granted the family of Prince d'Aragona Don Baldassare Naselli many special privileges, among which was the right of his male relations and retainers to carry any sort of arms, even if prohibited, a right which had been confirmed by subsequent monarchs. Sleeping dogs might have lain but for the fact that a scullery boy in the employ of Princess d'Aragona was arrested in possession of a prohibited weapon and Caracciolo had him flogged and exiled for five years, an event that aroused the wrath of the prince, since it infringed his centuries-old privileges. He appealed to the king. Again, one must emphasise that this was not a silly minor incident, but a matter of great import at the time. For Caracciolo, the incident was emblematic of the monstrosity of a fossilised system; for the barons, it was an outright attack on Sicilian traditions. The controversy continued for several months without solution before it dovetailed into the next incident, which concerned the same problem of the carrying of arms by privilege. In this instance, it was not a family that was involved, but an annual candlelit procession on the night of the Assumption by 23 guilds of craftsmen (who had the right to carry arms). Theoretically, the procession was illegal because there existed a royal decree stating that public processions after dinner were not allowed, but Caracciolo had been misinformed, by President Airoldi among others, that this event was acceptable, a fact which did not put him in a good mood. Caracciolo did not like religious processions at all, and he was not well disposed towards the craftsmen in general because of their past showing in the disturbances of 1773 and the fact that they depended structurally on the senate of Palermo, sometimes owed allegience to certain baronial families and were always a potential threat to public order. His worst fears were confirmed when a squabble about precedence broke out between the cheesemakers' and poulterers' guilds, which resulted in drawn swords, one death, two wounded and a public riot. He needed no better excuse than this for a formal request contained in a minute to Naples (22 August 1782)[15] that the procession be abolished and the number of guilds (which had grown to the excessive number of 74) be drastically reduced to a reasonable number of essential organisations. Apart from wishing to lessen the potential danger of the guilds, Caracciolo was also very interested in weakening the considerable powers of the *praetor* of Palermo, to whom ultimately the guilds responded. Caracciolo needed royal support because the interests were too entrenched; he wrote to Acton on 5 October 1782:

> If the King commands me ... and supports me I shall do it easily and make him really the Master of Palermo ... but I am not so silly as to take on such a task unless I can forsee an easy success.

Royal support was not expressed. While the D'Aragona case was being considered in Naples, yet another aspect of the question of arms carrying came up. It came to the viceroy's attention that many baronial families with the supposed right for their male offspring and servants to carry arms had arrogated the right to issue arms-licences to third parties under the false pretences that they were servants. Attached to his minute explaining the facts (10 October 1782) were two 'licences' issued by the Prince d'Aragona, explaining that not even the viceroy had the right to issue such documents. It was not until some time later, 26 December 1782, that satisfaction was received on this front: a proclamation was issued banning the wearing of swords, in Villabianca's words above all for 'the ordinary people, that is to say common people including servants and craftsmen in general both of the arts and the services.'[16] This may seem a small victory, but it was the establishment of the law of the state against the whim of privilege, reason over chaos, and the viceroy was seen to have won.

Some of the barons thought that their privilege allowed them freedom from prosecution. A case in point, one of many, was the un-named noble who found his magnificent country villa at Bagheria outside Palermo barred by the cavalry one day. In his anger, he turned to the viceroy, who received him immediately, asked if the villa was really his, and, receiving an affirmative answer, whether he had paid all the bills. The embarrassed 'owner' had to admit that he had not paid the architect, workmen or suppliers, at which point the viceroy informed him he would have access to the villa when he had done so.[17] The Duke of Sperlinga, on the other hand, had always led an unruly life well known to the authorities, but it became common knowledge that he had committed a murder on his feudal lands at Francavilla, suborned the local captain of police, intimidated witnesses and passed off the killing as an accident. When Caracciolo became aware of the details, he left no stone unturned until the duke was imprisoned in the castle at Milazzo and the captain of police and the other baronial legal officials ousted from their posts.[18]

Law and order, and indeed the workings of the law, were sorely tried by the episodes of violence involved in the *Marmorari* affair and its aftermath. Briefly what happened was this. Two marble-mason brothers called Palazzo killed a slave in a tavern brawl and, as was the custom at that time, they paid off the widow of the victim. Unfortunately, the slave was the property of the Marquis di Santa Croce, at the time the *Capitano di Giustizia*, who took the killing as an offence to his person and dignity and asked Caraccolo for the arrest of the siblings. The viceroy obviously agreed, but the barons and the populace did not, as this was going against custom. Overnight, the brothers became victims, and were taken up by public opinion. They turned outlaws and even had the audacity to stop Caracciolo's carriage one day as he was returning to Palermo from neighbouring Bagheria in order to explain their case to him, an act that failed miserably to convert him and indeed outraged him rather.[19] Soon after, the two were joined by a certain Rizzitello, and, as an armed band, committed a series of murders and pillages, including the killing of a judge and a young man in the service of a noble house. They even entered the city and shot off intimidating firearms at the house of the Marquis di Santa Croce. A large part of the populace was with them, but others were in panic; the police were powerless and the authorities in disrepute. At one point, the band were taken under the wing of the Prince of Pietraperzia (it was by no means unusual for the barons to give protection to bandits); apparently, he sent them for a time to Calabria, but on their return both they and the prince were arrested, the prince in a spectacular way. His arrest was, for most people at the time, astounding, since the area around his house was a no-go area. As Caracciolo wrote in a minute on 29 August 1782:

> [T]he guards and the agents of the magistrates, for the abuses that they find there, cannot, nor do they wish to go near the area where the Prince of Pietraperzia lives either to carry out some procedure of justice or to perform the night rounds; and however much I have strongly complained about this, admonishing the magistrates even, I have never been able to get them to act otherwise, such is their reluctance and fear.

The arrest of the prince was, therefore, theatrically public: the adjutant of the *Commandante delle Armi* was sent to his house, where the accused was packed into a coach and, accompanied by 24 grenadiers, driven off to the prison at the fort of Castellamare as an example to the population that the law was not to be tampered with. Public tension was very high, but Caracciolo had won the first round.

Successive bouts turned out to be more difficult. The three ringleaders, the *Marmorari*, came up for trial before a court presided over by Airoldi and other judges in whom Caracciolo had more faith, but the fact was that, thanks to Airoldi's influence, only one of the brothers was condemned to death while the other two defendants were given relatively light sentences, an outcome that enraged the viceroy. He swamped Naples with documents concerning the case, including the sentences given by the judges, and had this to say about Airoldi: 'It seemed to me a declaration in favour of the criminals and not a reasonable sentence', appearing to be asking for greater support from Naples in view of the prince's approaching case.

The prince's case took a long time and involved a point of law that Caracciolo felt had great significance for a wider field of justice, and which needs some explanation. It had been usual in important, sensitive cases of law like this one for the viceroy, even in conjunction with the parties, to appoint two adjunct judges to assist regular judges in the process of examining the case and judging it. Over time it had become the custom before the choice of the adjuncts was made to draw up 'tables of *suspect* and *non-suspect* judges', and when it came to choosing the adjunct judges in cases that concerned them personally the barons chose them from the *tavola dei non sospetti* with complete confidence because they had taken care to select only names obedient to their interests for inclusion on the list. Such was the system.[20] Pietraperzia claimed the right to reject the adjunct judges the viceroy was proposing. Caracciolo replied that according to a decree of 1780 the 'table of *suspect* and *non-suspect* judges' could only be applied in cases between contending civil parties and not in cases between the government and a civil party, when the civil party had no right of rejection of the adjunct judge, though he could, of course, apply for his removal through the normal channels, if just causes could be proven. Caracciolo's legal mind was challenged. He wrote to Minister De Marco in Naples:

> Either by the trickery of litigants or the negligence of magistrates ... Your Excellency must clearly realize that there

exists no law of the kingdom that lays down the necessity of the tables, that their use is tantamount to subverting one of the most sacrosanct rights of sovereignty.[21]

He was concerned with the wider issue of justice, but this was a problem that the legal minds in Naples needed time to sort out, as it was one that had repercussions that went well beyond Pietraperzia's case, who in the meantime remained in prison. Caracciolo continued to argue his case hotly with Naples in a series of minutes that flowed from Palermo. So concerned, however, was he with the question of justice that when he was informed officially that the affair should proceed 'according to the usages and laws of the Kingdom' (that is to say, he was overruled) he suspended the case on his own initiative and awaited further orders, maintaining that sometimes central government did not quite understand local legislation and needed more time. On 22 March 1782 the question was ominously turned over to the *Giunta di Sicilia* in Naples (a notorious hotbed of Sicilian conservatism) and the prince was complaining to the king about his prolonged incarceration.[22] The case was not finally solved, and that very unsatisfactorily for Caracciolo, until 5 May 1783, when the *Giunta di Sicilia* pronounced on the use of the 'table of judges' and the case of Pietraperzia. The *Giunta*, which was at pains to explain how 'Sicilian' it was, after hypocritically admiring the marquis's zeal and his commendable commitment to the correct and impartial administration of Justice, plumped solidly for the use of the 'tables' as an ancient usage that had only been very minutely altered by the decree of 1780 and not so as to make it inapplicable in the case in point, so that Pietraperzia was right and the viceroy wrong. Needless to say, Villabianca and the barons were brimful of glee. It is interesting to quote Villabianca's opinion on the case:

But then Pietrperzia's crime was a simple act of protection, which is after all innate in the souls of great lords; and so his case did not merit being considered so criminal as to hold one of the first lords of Sicily in gaol for one year and a month.[23]

Caracciolo's fury was intense, but conservatism, the system and, it must be said, the king's indecision had blocked the viceroy's will for change. At the time, however, his mind was probably more bound up with the question of tax reform.

But this was in the future. While he was dealing with the *Mamorari* affair he was contemplating other ways of bringing the Sicilian government to heel, some of them decidedly radical. At the beginning of October 1782 he announced to the governor of Messina his intention of moving his court and all his offices to that city from the following spring, making it the capital of the Kingdom of Sicily in the hope that new life and commercial activity would be injected into it.[24] This was not an idle threat of the moment: he had been considering such a move for some time. In his first recorded letter to Acton on 27 June 1782 he had written that of the two or three great operations needed to 're-order Sicily', which seemed impossible, but were in fact very straightforward, 'one would be, for example, that the viceroy with the tribunals and the whole shop should go for three years to Messina'.[25] Caracciolo was genuinely interested in the fortunes of this city, which was on the decline and not contributing to the treasury as he thought it could have in different circumstances, though of course he was also very keen on shaking the pretensions of Palermo. But the disastrous major earthquake that struck Messina the following year meant he was not able to develop this idea any further, if indeed he were to have been allowed to do so.

In less radical mode, in around about this period, Caracciolo managed to find the time to reform the system of water distribution in Palermo (some of the officials had been fraudulently selling water to the public for their private gain), and also the *Capitani di Giustizia*, the abysmally paid nightwatchmen, whom he enabled to be paid properly by state funds. He also began to busy himself with the fact that the post office did not belong to the state: the throne had ceded it to the Prince of Villafranca and his family in 1734. He found that the service left much to be desired, but that there was very little he could do about this due to its private status. For example, he often had to use special couriers for delicate matters, which was costly – this was a recurring theme in his correspondence with Naples, the first recorded letter being dated 26 August 1782.[26]

During this time Caracciolo had also been working on his aforementioned plan for a public cemetery outside the walls of Palermo, against the public opinion of all classes. The first stone was laid on 21 April 1783.

Meanwhile, the question of the *catasto* still remained unanswered. This problem had never left Caracciolo's mind for an instant while all these other issues had been on his desk; it was central to everything he hoped to do in Sicily. However, while waiting for the king to pronounce on the Demesnial chamber's request concerning the new census during the last *Parlamento*, he had not been idle. He assumed that the king had given him *carte blanche* to study the best way of implementing a new census, though in reality the sovereign probably intended a rather more prudent use of the processes traditionally followed where major Sicilian questions were concerned.[27] Nonetheless, Caracciolo began work on a detailed plan with Simonetti and two other ministers. He told Acton so that it could be submitted to the king, but he made a point of not telling anybody else. He had also asked Simonetti to produce another *Consulta* looking at why the barons paid nothing at all towards the thirteen ordinary *donativi*. This new *Consulta* (28 December 1782), apart from dealing with that fiscal immunity, gave a full tax history of Sicily, killing the myth of military service in lieu of taxes. And while he waited for a royal decision, Caracciolo plied Acton with letter after letter in favour of the decision he wanted: you mustn't smell medicines, but swallow them, he urged; the Milan census inspired by Pompeo Neri and introduced by the Empress Maria Teresa was easy to implement and did such good, he pronounced; don't listen to the *Deputazione del Regno* because it is not impartial, he warned; I shall send Simonetti to Naples and he can explain it to the *Deputazione*, he stressed – and so on and so on. It was clear that he was trying to put his point of view directly to the king, via Acton, without involving any of the constitutional instruments of Sicily. But what was really worrying Caracciolo was a royal change of mind – 'the voluble change that often occurs in royal determinations makes me tremble.'[28] The Decision *must* come soon.

10

Broadside

✦✦✦✦✦

A personal letter at this time to an old friend, Angelo Fabbroni,[1] is worth quoting in full as it expresses many of Caracciolo's private feelings, and, though he goes through the various public works that he has been able to put into motion, he significantly spares his literary friend the torment of the *catasto* problem, which was undoubtedly gnawing at his bowels at the time. The missive was written from Palermo on 19 June 1783:

> I received your much esteemed letter of the 19th March and, since it is such a pleasure to see oneself in the memory of one's friends, you may imagine what a pleasure it was to receive it, coming as it did from a person whom I esteem, love and honour; I am indeed indebted. It displeased me however that you made use of titles and compliments – another time please confine them to the profane envelope so that the body of the letter remains sacred to friendship and cordiality.
>
> Oh! How it consoled me to be remembered *sur les arides bordes de la sauvage Sicile*. My dear friend, I have been condemned to lick this bear; I have already managed to destroy the terrible monster of the Inquisition and to bestow liberty on the sale of foodstuffs, to initiate and develop urban streets and to work on roads in the Kingdom, but then there are infinities of things remaining to do and other monsters

still to slay. I am no Hercules and what makes every task even more difficult is the resistance that comes from those whom one is trying to deliver from the tyranny of the powerful – such is the extent a long bondage *degrade l'ame* that it no longer feels the weight of the chains. I am building a fine theatre here for the living and a cemetery for the dead; this latter was suggested to me by those I saw in Pisa and Livorno, but this one here is big and will be common to all without exception. Palermo has a large population; with its suburbs and environs it amounts to 250 thousand inhabitants; and it is very tightly closed within the city walls; in the summer the churches smell unbearably and these barbarians were quite happy to go about in the smell under the burning sky.

The cemetery I have planned is about a mile from the city on a small hill which is reached by a road flanked with trees. At the top of the hill there is a large walled square with four great doors in the four sides which give onto 200 arches per side that form porticos 12 feet wide; behind each arch there is a chapel and a tomb; in front of each portico there is space for 360 tombs for the populace, where the poor will be buried without funereal expenses. The wherewithal for the annual maintenance costs has been found from certain useless suppressed confraternities; the first income for such a large undertaking, which will cost 100 thousand scudi without imposing on the government, came from the concession of the said chapels, many of which were taken up by noble houses for their families, and also by all the convents and monasteries, the craft organisations etc: and each of them has to take care of all of the construction at its own expense to acquire ownership and the cost comes to about 250 scudi for each arch, chapel and tomb. Only the archbishop, parish priests and nuns are exempted from burial in the cemetery. The barons can be carried to their feudal lands, if they so desire, otherwise to the cemetery like all the others. My friend, this good that I try to do for humanity comforts me, and consoles me for the pain of being forced away from Paris to Palermo.

Let us now address our affairs. I am happy to hear that you proceed in your very useful work concerning the lives of illustrious Italians, a work I believe will be both pleasurable and instructive. The history of those that we should take as models for their spirit and for the cleansing of our souls I consider fine moral painting for our youth. Above all it gives me pleasure to know you are occupying yourself with Lorenzo Il Magnifico, an outstanding man in his time. I have many times wished for a history of Leo X's century which would begin with the fall of Constantinople and end with the conclusion of The Council of Trent. There is no literary history of Italy, nor a Saracen history and it would also be useful to know what increase and progress the sciences had in the hands of the Arabs, who maintained them in the tenth century while we were in the depths of darkness. A copy of your work, as of anything you produce, would be highly appreciated by me, if you remember me in these far frontiers of Christianity.

I shall not speak to you of politics, as I have forgotten about them in the great Sicilian vacuum that reigns here concerning such subjects; however it appears to me that Russian gentlemen are learning the Mediterranean road overmuch, none of us are circulating in the Baltic, each of us should stay at home. Poor D'Alembert is afflicted with a bladder complaint, I get continuous letters about it and the fact afflicts me a great deal as well, because I love him as my own brother and in the last period of my stay in Paris we were inseparable; his complaint is serious and painful and he has not the courage to endure it, though he is not at all afraid of death; he is deserving of pity; death should not cause fear in a wise man, but to finish in pain is a cruelty.

Vale amicissimum caput. Command me if I can be of any service to you here; preserve your friendship for me, and let Heaven preserve you always for happy futures.

That was a pleasant aside to an old friend: political life in *sauvage Sicile* was not proving as easy as reason had led Caracciolo to believe. Nature itself seemed to be against him. On 8 February 1783 a courier arrived in Palermo with the news of the Messina earthquake that had hit the town on the fifth and the seventh – the tremors having been previously felt in the capital – killing, Villabianca registered, 617 people. Palermo and Naples were galvanised into doing what they could, but the destruction was complete, and, of course, Caracciolo's plan for moving the capital there came to nothing. The ensuing economic, social and even political problems were considerable. They coincided with the first judgement on the Pietraperzia case, when Caracciolo postponed accepting it on the basis that the *Giunta di Sicilia* in Naples was ignorant of local customs in Sicily, but above all the quake and its aftermath came at the time Caracciolo was waiting for The Decision on the *catasto*, pestering Acton, his chief support in Naples, with letters and the publication of Simonetti's *Consulte*.

It soon became clear that money would have to be raised for the reconstruction of Messina, that this would have to be done through *Parlamento*, and that the question would become embroiled in the debate on his fundamental policy of tax reform. On 13 March 1783 Caracciolo was writing to Acton about the central government's plans for the reconstruction of Messina[2] with which he thoroughly agreed: he hoped that the works would be carried out to the advantage 'not only of Sicily, but of the Kingdom of Naples', given the importance and the geographical position of the city, and stressed that such a large operation should be judged not in its details but in the larger scheme of things, which gave him the opening to re-introduce the subject closest to his heart:

> I make these reflections, which may be painful to you. I am very fearful for the *catasto*; they will turn it around and around until it falls to the ground. These rather arduous and elevated affairs are like medicines, when you smell them and sniff them too long it appears difficult to swallow them.

He went on to say that the opinion of the *Deputazione del Regno* would never be unbiased and that the new tax system was entirely feasible. Three days later he was lecturing Acton on Maria Theresa's *catasto* and taxation, which was introduced with success into the Duchy of Milan in 1750 in the face of similar problems, and the process continued. In the meantime the chief minister in Naples, the Sicilian Marchese di Sambuca, had sent an official to the island to organise the raising of an extraordinary tax for the relief of Messina. Caracciolo, writing to Acton on 17 April 1783, explains how even some members of *Parlamento* who had on other occasions been unwilling to submit to the tax (naming names) were now willing to pay and that the figure that they had come up with (without his suggesting it) was 400,000 *scudi* payable over 4 years, in equal parts (he hoped) by the barons, the ecclesiastics and the Demesne ... But he had his doubts. Had they zealously offered to pay in equal parts just 'to avoid any danger of [*catasto*] reform'? The doubt was legitimate.

Caracciolo's next attempt to apply reason, as he saw it, to human affairs was an unmitigated disaster: he decided to reform the festivities of Santa Rosalia, the patron Saint of Palermo. He did not like religious processions or crowds generally, as they were a potential source of tumults, remembering the Cerei affair and the problem of armed craftsmen. He thought the enormous effort expended on the Santa Rosalia a terrible waste, so he ordered the *praetor* on 4 June 1783 to reduce the festivities from five days to three and devote the money saved to charity. There was, of course, outrage, and the *praetor* and senate refused to carry out his orders. On 10 June he wrote ingenuously to Acton about how dissolutely, expensively and profanely the five days were normally spent and how 'against all my expectations' the senate, the *praetor* and the mayor of the city were opposed to his 'holy' plan. It hardly seems likely that Caracciolo thought he could get off lightly with a move that unpopular and he certainly did not: Villabianca's diaries express some of the aristocratic disdain, while popular outrage was vividly captured in graffiti daubed near Caracciolo's apartments in the Viceregal Palace: '*O Festa o testa*' ('The *Festa* or your head'). The court at Naples was deluged with appeals and petitions to save the beloved festival and the king's sentence was awaited with bated breath.

Preoccupation with tax reform remained paramount, but Caracciolo was also worried that if the extraordinary tax for Messina were somehow to be used

> as a motive, pretext and excuse for postponing or even dropping the now well known Project for the Enumeration and Valuation of the landed property of Sicily then I consider it, the above mentioned *Donativo* [the Messina tax], fatal to this Kingdom and to the service of the King.[3]

In the same letter he went on to explain that he was worried because he had heard nothing of the project for some time and had heard a lot of the 'Sicilian cabal', which was having a whale of a time in Naples over the Santa Rosalia affair. He was probably right: while he had been working behind the backs of the Sicilian barons trying to get the king to approve his proposals for the Plan, they had voluntarily, cleverly and substantially behind his back proposed the donation to the king of 400,000 *scudi* for the damage done to the kingdom by the Messina earthquake. Political finesse was always Caracciolo's weak point.

With this very much in mind he set about organising the extraordinary *Parlamento*, which was constitutionally necessary to authenticate the extraordinary Messina tax that had been agreed in March. Before it assembled, the *Deputazione del Regno* met, without Caracciolo's knowledge, and decided that the *donativo* should be divided equally between the three *Braccie*, or chambers of *Parlamento*: however, behind the scenes and without the deputies of the Demesnial chamber being present, the other two chambers, together with the *Deputazione*, decided that the Demesnial chamber would, as usual, pay the lion's share[4] – a result of a series of category deductions they agreed on secretly.

Caracciolo got wind of what was going on. *Parlamento* met on 30 June 1783. The fact should not be overlooked (and the barons certainly did not turn a blind eye) that Caracciolo had his secretary Gargano and friends of his (among whom Emmanuele Lo Castro, who acted in favour of the government, was prominent) elected to the Demesne chamber, though it has to be said this move had precedents in viceregal history: he did not know officially what had happened behind the scenes at the *Deputazione del Regno*, but, as has been already said, he had been informed and had a good idea that a move was underway to outmanoeuvre his plan for the new *catasto*.

Caracciolo's opening speech when *Parlamento* met was aggressive and so clear that it was considered lacking in respect by his audience. He made it obvious that he expected the *donativo* to be equally divided between the three chambers of the *Parlamento* without any subterfuge on the part of the barons and ecclesiastics to the detriment of the Demesne and justice generally and made it equally transparent that the government would be particularly vigilant in view of the future tax reforms. All sides took uncompromising positions: the barons and the ecclesiastics defended their constitutional right to divide up the taxes as they wished, refused to consider tax reform and petitioned the king against viceregal abuse of power; the Demesne chamber petitioned the king against the unjust division of the taxes, which left them paying for almost all of it. Caracciolo accepted the *donativo* in the name of the king, but refused the division as unjust, awaited a royal decision, and terminated the *Parlamento*. According to Villabianca,

> each of the barons and all of the other parliamentarians returned promptly to their houses murmuring bitterly against the villainous and despicable methods of governor Caracciolo.[5]

Petitions poured into Naples from all sources. What happened emerges perhaps best from two descriptive letters that Caracciolo sent Acton on 3 and 10 July 1783.[6] This is what transpired.

When he had first negotiated the *donativo* in March he had been surprised that everything had gone so quickly and so well, but Simonetti, the *consultore*, a man of 'discriminating nose' (*emunctae naris*), noticed some smallprint in the general terms that mentioned 'certain deductions' before the division of the *donativo*, though not too much attention was paid to this at the time. However, when, on the evening of 2 July 1783, the three chambers met formally to agree on the division of the 400,000 *scudi*, the deductions that applied to the barons and the ecclesiastics were calculated (the tax on Palermo, Mortmain, i.e. all the monasteries and convents, all non-baronial titles, all freemen and people with privileges in the kingdom, all the tradespeople of Sicily), and it was revealed that these two chambers should pay only 77,000 *scudi* each (rather than 133,000) with all the rest falling to the Demesne chamber.

Caracciolo's reaction was unsurprising: he had been formally expecting an equal division and had been telling the government to expect as such, so this move came in for heavy treatment in a letter to Acton. Among other things, he pointed out that, apart from being extremely unjust, a fiscal system of this type was also extremely inefficient and that Sicily could easily provide a third more to the treasury if it were better administered. His secretary, Gargano, made a compromise proposal – that the barons and ecclesiastics should pay 101,000 *scudi* instead of 77,000 – but they would have none of it. This was an extra reason, Caracciolo told Acton, why he refused to accept the division. The political infighting was intense. Despite aristocratic leadership of the Demesne chamber, which was favourable towards acceptance of the views of the barons and the ecclesiastics, there was a revolt within the body of the assembly, organised by Emmanuele Lo Castro, which gained followers for a petition to the king against the injustice of the division of the *donativo* and the insistence of the other two chambers in moving the division without the backing of the Demesne (also Caracciolo's position, but actually quite constitutional) and in favour of the tax reform. Meanwhile, the other two chambers were supplicating the king via the *Deputazione del Regno* to send a deputy to plead their case: they were against the tax reform, they felt they had been betrayed by the viceroy in that they had indicated on the 16 April the deductions that they were going to make to the *donativo*, the same as those that had been made by the *Parlamento* of 1746, and above all the considered *Parlamento* had been inopportunely menaced and protested by Caracciolo's opening speech rather than being treated with the respect it merited. A memorial from the *Deputazione* even suggested that a first payment of the *donativo* could have been made as early as August had it not been for the

> inopportune zeal and impetuous conduct in public affairs and
> blind condescension to other people's suggestions [which had

given rise to] the most intense sense of disgust, regret and bitter sorrow on the part of the promoters of the *Donativo*.[7]

They also accused Lo Castro of extorting signatures and disturbing the kingdom, the viceroy of being unable to accept a *donativo* and refuse the methods of its division, while maintaining that it was their privilege to distribute *donativi*. Caracciolo was not to be outdone in the controversy: it was imperative the government win, and he implored Acton to intercede 'with your usual force and energy' with the sovereigns 'in favour of this poor country ... making use of all your zeal ... for the salvation of Sicily'. But everything took time with the king, who was a conservative and not much interested in politics anyway.

In the meantime the festival of Santa Rosalia was not a moveable feast and a decision had to be made. A royal despatch was sent off from Naples on 28 June 1783 and arrived in Palermo on 6 July. 'While admiring the zeal that has been applied to this reform', the compliment came with the proviso that 'at some time in the future what may be considered opportune concerning this affair of the *festa*' would be re-examined. It laid down that 'meanwhile for this year it should be observed as it is normally, without the introduction of any novelties'. The crowds were beside themselves with joy at the news, as were all the aristocrats, and the *festa* was carried out with much pomp and circumstance, mirth and waste[8] over the full five days.

It became increasingly clear to the viceroy that the success of his reforms in Sicily depended on the full backing of the king in Naples, who was being lobbied behind his back by the 'Sicilian party', which was undermining his authority and hence sovereignty. In various letters on 17 July 1783[9] Caracciolo dealt with the problem at length, beginning with unjust complaints from the *Deputazione del Regno* about Lo Castro (who had protested to the king in the name of the Demesne chamber about the division of the tax), which he described to Marchese Sambuca as 'impertinent.' To Acton, he wrote that he should note the obstinacy of the deputation and not revert to the old, arbitrary taxes so damaging to the poor townships, and that the sovereigns must be talked to clearly and convinced that the barons must not be allowed to continue in their privileges:

> If your Excellency with your zeal and firmness does not speak with frankness to the Patrons [the sovereigns] and explain that, if they let these gentlemen do what they will, the King will remain Patron in name alone in Sicily, I shall wash my hands of the affair: I have said it, I say it, and I repeat it, as far as I am concerned I have done my duty. This is not a joke, we are not dealing with the *festa* of Santa Rosalia. This is a question of Sovereign Rights of the first order, the happiness of the Kingdom, half a million more in fiscal revenue which a well-administered Sicily can render without further burdening the Nation.

That he was not receiving the backing he ought to have had from the king in Naples in his confrontation with the Sicilian baronage was an impression that did not leave Caracciolo and fed increasing thoughts of retirement over the next few months, though one must not underestimate that he had never been used to the rough and tumble of political life and was 68 years old, a considerable age at the time. On 24 July[10] he wrote a vigorous rebuttal of the document sent to the government in Naples setting out *Parlamento*'s view of the distribution of the *donativo*, a document Caracciolo rightly pointed out was illegal, as all correspondence with the government in Naples had to go through his office. It contained an analysis of the 1746 deductions the barons were using as a precedent and which had been drafted 'by the Prince of Trabia with such effrontery, or, better perhaps, by others under his name, because he is an imbecile.' The letter is long, explains the complicated question of the deductions in great detail and announces the departure of Simonetti, the *consultore*, for Naples the next day to make sure that the government had somebody available who really knew what the facts and the situation were. It was vital for Caracciolo to have Simonetti in Naples: he was always convinced that the 'Sicilian cabal' had packed the court and isolated the king, making it almost impossible for his voice to get through. With Simonetti in Naples things would be easier. His correspondence with Naples always harked on this lack of clear communication, but the tone grew strident now: it was not that his projects were not reasonable and just or that the king was not wise and benevolent, just that between them there was a rabble of interfering, obscurantist, Sicilian barons. This insistence on his point of view being understood clearly by the court, both with regard to the Messina *donativo* and with the larger question of the general *catasto* reform, was hammered home in letter after letter and cannot have been light reading for Acton.

About this time Caracciolo began to hint officially that he was considering retirement. On 17 August[11] he wrote that he was highly upset that his secretary, Gargano, was being attacked by the barons for doing his duty (he had been elected to represent the cities of Messina and Catania, and had spoken up for them in *Parlamento*). Not only was Gargano his secretary, but he was honest and Neapolitan, whereas the rich and powerful in Sicily only wanted corruptible people in the administration and government in their own way:

> It is tough to combat with the Sicilians, but it becomes unbearable and a torment difficult to put into words, to have to combat at Naples as well ... Well, then, I'll go, I do not at all

want to stay in Sicily, I am not looking for anything in Naples ... I hope the charity of the King will allow me a crust of bread and treat me as pensioner after thirty-four years of service. In any case I prefer begging to being Viceroy of Sicily; at least I shall live quietly and without the risk of one day or other being dishonoured, affronted, put on trial. *Absit!* There have been so many shots fired that one of these days one will land, and, to tell you the truth, Gargano's case has put me in the mind to depart: *Fuge crudeles terras et littus avarum!*

While this was clearly not a formal offer of resignation, it was a sign of some considerable depression, and in his next letter to Acton on 21 August 1783 Caracciolo was having to defend himself from claims that, in refusing the division of the *donativo*, he had in effect refused in the king's name the *donativo* itself. He returned briefly but with more optimism to the subject in a letter dated 11 September 1783:[12]

Hence it is very difficult to battle in Sicily and in Naples; I find it beyond my energies and it weakens my steadfastness; nonetheless, even though I am very indifferent about leaving this office and have no other idea than to retire, my heart cannot accept the sad idea of losing all my past services and of exiting dishonourably from the King's service after thirty-four years of toil; in fact it is a cruelty that my zeal in serving the Sovereign and the State should, by the wretchedness of ambitious and dishonest people, be transformed into a demerit and shame on my part. However, under the good auspices of that most clement of Lady Patrons, *Flos Reginarum*, I now live in more security and tranquillity; I am assured not a little courage and good spirit also from Your Excellency's honourable protection as revealed in your last two confidential letters of the 23 September and the 30 August.

The point here was that he had the queen's ear and therefore could bypass the Sicilian cabal. The queen was very active in government and Acton was particularly close her at this time (some say her lover).

Caracciolo reactivated his administrative defences. He re-issued his December 1781 *circolare* whereby all communication with the court at Naples had to pass through the viceregal offices so that the infiltration of subterfuges might be nipped in the bud, and he stamped, with varying success, on officials bound to their noble protectors who did not carry out his orders to perfection, especially those who had been beguiled with small favours and easy promises to propagate false information. These moves on Caracciolo's part created a reaction from the barons that resulted in complaints in the *Corte di Napoli* (not the royal court), a minor court where they were able to elude the viceroy and make 'humble supplications' to be liberated from a 'slavery harsher than that of the People of Israel in Babilonia' and legislation harder than that of the Ottomans'.[13] The barons were at work at other levels, as indeed was Caracciolo, who had Simonetti, armed with his *Voto* (a codification of Sicily's fiscal history and Caracciolo's case history in favour of the Crown versus the Barons), as his sitting representative at Naples.

After 'mature consideration', a decision was arrived at on the question of the Messina *donativo* and transmitted via the *Supremo Consiglio di Finanze* on 20 September 1783. It judged that the complaint of the Demesne chamber was 'without foundation' and that its calculation 'to reduce its contribution to a lower sum' was 'irregular and capricious', that it accepted the offer of 400,000 *scudi* 'and also the division already agreed upon by the two Chambers, the Baronial and Ecclesiastical', conceding the liberty to the demesnial townships to 'appeal to the Throne in legitimate forms'.[14] Although Lo Castro was acquitted (as having acted under viceregal orders) and no formal reference was made to the general tax reform, the barons had won handsomely, and the viceroy was 'humiliated'.

In a letter to Acton dated 2 October 1783 and in another, presumably closely connected, undated one, Caracciolo explained his position. He realised that the decision could not have been otherwise 'since it was necessary to give execution to the *donativo*, but the paint that was unnecessarily brushed over it offends truth, justice and charity; leaving the Viceroy furthermore unreasonably humiliated'. His first reaction, he said, was to protest to the king that this was a blow to the Plan for tax reform, but 'I judged it better to suffer the situation in peace ... and not convenient ... to play the Don Quixote of the Demesne Chamber of the Sicilian Parlamento.'

The Sicilian cabal, which included Prime Minister Sambuca, was not only plotting in Naples but also in Madrid against the Plan. The barons were laughing over their first victory and thinking about their next, far more important, one, and so was Caracciolo, contemplating a Sicily that was in complete economic ruin:

> Now that I have done my duty with all the strength of my mind and spirit, and perhaps done more than another in my place would have done, whatever is the outcome of the new Plan, I shall not say another word, neither for good nor for ill.[15]

He did not, of course, keep to his word, and Simonetti remained in Naples as his very able mouthpiece.

It should be noted that Lo Castro was acquitted because it was recognised that he had been acting under orders from the viceroy. Caracciolo, as has been seen, was also extremely energetic in his defence of his secretary, Gargano, who had been severely attacked by the opposition for his part in the Demesne chamber's activities, and wrote several spirited detailed letters to Acton vindicating his actions.[16] He had few close collaborators, but he was very loyal to them. Simonetti could do no wrong.

In the meantime he turned his immediate energies to public issues, concentrating on the streets of Palermo, the restoration of its cathedral, the consolidation of the cemetery, the construction of a new theatre, the re-structuring of various piazzas and roads and the demolition of some useless bastions of privilege. This rush of new activity was generally appreciated (even by Villabianca)[17] and confined to Palermo, the centre of baronial influence, in an attempt to create new work and a new sense of industriousness. There were, of course, clashes with noble proprietors, parts of whose houses were in the way of the new piazzas, but stirring things up and destroying inertia was part of Caracciolo's thinking. Housing outside the walls of the city was encouraged and the theatre itself was planned to be outside the *Porta Maqueda.*

It was also evident to the viceroy, who was a genuine eighteenth-century economist, how all the major and most profitable Sicilian industries, such as they were, were either in foreign or aristocratic hands, or both. A glaring case in point was the post office whose de-privatisation Caracciolo had been insistently recommending to the king for some time. The postal service had passed to the Prince of Villafranca in 1734 by royal grant, ever since which there had been complaints of delays and bad service. Caracciolo himself had told the court in 1782 that he was forced to use private couriers for security reasons, and at other times that he considered the loss to the revenue a disgrace.[18] Finally, in September 1783, Sambuca sent him an urgent and reserved brief in the name of the king to ask what should be done. The answer was succinct: there were few complaints to the existing system because the family was generous if the complainers were important, the rates were far too reasonable because they wished to avoid attention ('they had not wanted to endow a beautiful girl with a rich dowry so that she should not become the more desirable and sought-after'), and all that was needed for the king to take over the system was to increase the tariffs and gain prestige and considerable fiscal revenue and to pay back 'the sum that the gentleman has paid out'.[19] This was described as a 'tenuous sum' when compared with the 'very enormous damage that [Villafranca's ownership of the post office] caused the Kingdom' in a legal document that Caracciolo had prepared and sent to Naples.[20]

Even though the question was urgent and reserved, the prince was aware of what was afoot and urging his side of the affair.[21] Caracciolo was informed that 'at a further date the final royal decisions would be communicated' – decisions he would wait for in vain for the whole of the rest of his time in Sicilian office. Nothing was touched, nothing was changed: here was the totally irresolute royal decree that Caracciolo was beginning to anticipate and fear, a tangible sign that he was not getting the support he needed from Naples to do what needed to be done. The fact was that the king had no intention of stirring things up. As befitted his nature, Caracciolo did not let the matter drop: his letters to Acton continued to harp on the matter, and included a comment that letters were opened not even for reasons of state, but for pure curiosity (undated but presumably late January 1784[22]) and a proposal to the king for a very advantageous loan so that he could buy out postmaster Villafranca (4 December 1784[23]).

Fighting against the Sicilian cabal on the political front was not enough and Caracciolo now turned his attention to the printed word. He was determined to make sure that publications contrary to the ideas behind his policies did not see the light of day, to say nothing of those that propagated false information and propaganda against the Plan. A band was issued on 4 November 1783 that outlawed the printing and publishing of all books and writings within the Kingdom of Sicily that did not have viceregal permission. On the same date he signed a circolare that withdrew the right of the president of the *Gran Corte* to issue the *publietur*, the licence to publish he had hitherto enjoyed. Caracciolo also published and circulated towards the end of October a manifesto by which 'the public was informed of the reasonableness of his projects', and he also had printed a *Discorso Istruttivo* and a *Piano Dimostrativo*, which he 'spread around Sicily' and of which he sent many copies to Naples so that everybody could have the matter under discussion in their hands, could see the truth, and could appreciate the advantages and goodness of the proposed new system,[24] demonstrating a truly eighteenth-century belief in reason though not in tolerance … and far too late. He was not an astute politician.

Caracciolo asked that the garrison at Palermo should be reinforced by one or two battalions, not from fear of an uprising of the people, but for reasons of prestige more than anything else. He deemed the present military presence too small and undistinguished for a city of 250,000 people. There was also the fact that a detachment had to be sent to Messina, where it was really needed by the unfortunate inhabitants – there were disorders caused by the soldiers themselves and by escaping convicts, who stole all they could lay their hands on, even the iron railings from the balconies and anything else they could transport away. Caracciolo wanted to impose martial law on Messina and to begin organising it after the earthquake now that the tax had been arranged. He was full of plans for reviving its economy without the aristocratic cabal that characterised Palermo.

Despite telling Acton that he would not say another word about the Plan, Caracciolo continued to ply Naples with pressure for what he knew was in the best interests of Sicily and hence the Kingdom of the Two Sicilies, and at a time when he was growing tired and ill. There is considerable correspondence all to the effect that unless the reform went through the people of Sicily would suffer, and

> I am neutral, a younger son, with no property in Sicily or in Naples. I seek nothing; I desire nothing better than retirement when the King in his infinite mercy restores me my liberty and grants me a piece of bread to eat on the plain of Sorrento. For the rest I wash my hands like Pilate.

Depression gave way to renewed energy, however, when there was a chance to undermine the privileges of the barons. A striking example was Caracciolo's brush at the end of 1783 with the head of the Geraci-Ventimiglia family, whose exalted sense of importance included the assumed privilege of excluding the whole family from all public offices, and the styling of his own titles – preceded by 'by the Grace of God' – including 'First Count of Italy', 'First Lord of the One and the Other Sicily' and 'Prince of the Holy Roman Empire' (an honour to which he was not entitled). Caracciolo promptly appointed the prince's eldest son a senator of Palermo; his father thereupon sent him on holiday to the mainland, whereupon the viceroy sent the father a despatch annulling his pompous titles, a despatch that was delivered by the fiscal advocate in person, formally accompanied by officials of the *Gran Corte*.[25] The scandal was enormous. Once again, although this might seem a piece of musical comedy, it was a serious attempt to re-dimension the absurd privileges of the barons that reflected badly on the prestige of the viceregal government: Caracciolo devoted nearly two letters to Acton on the subject.[26] However, he did not receive the backing he needed, as the king reconfirmed all the titles, except 'by the Grace of God'. Once again, it is most interesting to hear Villabianca's opinion on this controversy.[27] He began by saying that it was in the court's interest to beat down the barons because they were *comillitones* according to the Di Napoli theory previously discussed, during Count Roger's invasion of Sicily against the Saracens, and therefore their legitimate and not feudal power was seen as a threat to the court at Naples. He then went on to talk of the house of Ventimiglia di Geraci, which had some claim to the throne of Sicily through a very distant link with the Norman royal family: the present small and suspicious Neapolitan court wished to humiliate the whole of the Sicilian baronage by putting down this family. He also said that the Marquis of Geraci met the Emperor of Germany in January 1784 in Naples to negotiate the restitution of his titles.

Another substantial blow against baronial privilege, however, was dealt on 13 February 1784, a *Prammatica* that laid down in absolute terms that no baronial judge could exercise both civil and criminal jurisdictions in either baronial or crown townships. That was bad enough, but what caused even more chagrin with the barons was a band issued on the same date, occasioned by the fact that Caracciolo had noted 'the elections of officials in baronial lands were not carried out according to the norms of the law nor did they always fall on able people'. From now onwards elections were to take place every year on the first day of September and a person could not be nominated for an office unless he had not held it for at least two years.[28] Caracciolo reformed the elections in the same way for the captains, judges and *giurati* (public officials) in both baronial and crown townships, so that the barons could not get their hands on the public revenues. There was a great outcry on the part of the barons about these two measures and in a letter to Acton at the time (14 February 1784)[29] Caracciolo once again expressed his lack of optimism in the king's will to back him up resolutely:

> Two Circolari have broken the chains of the inhabitants here, and the name of His Majesty who has given them force and sanction is everywhere blessed ... It now remains, my Excellent

Lord, that the Law should remain in place; already these gentlemen, by means of their subterfuges, have moved to have it withdrawn, and I tremble to receive one day or another a Despatch saying that it has been revised, and the phoenix will rise from the ashes again.

Sicilians (barons, to all intents and purposes) were also disallowed from acting as consuls or viceconsuls around this time.[30] Caracciolo also noted in a letter to Acton[31] that the barons not only did not raise the images of the sovereigns on their lands on festive occasions, but actually had their own images raised instead. Caracciolo quite rightly considered this a very serious matter, not simply a question of pomp and circumstance. For him, it amounted to a question of *lèse-majesté*, if not declaration of Sicilian independence. He therefore issued a *circolare* that banned this awful abuse and ordered the showing of the images of the sovereigns to 'put before the eyes of the people the figure of the real Patron so that they should know from whom only they should look for hope'. It should be noted that a year later he was again writing to Acton to inform him that baronial images were still being raised by various grand families (Butera, Cattolica and Modica), arrogantly ignoring his orders,[32] and explaining how he had issued a new *circolare* against the baronial prisons:

[I]t is their custom to keep a sort of pit, into which they lower their miserable vassals by means of a rope; I have therefore – since these prisons are against the Laws, both for charitable reasons and for reasons of piety towards poor humanity – ordered the *Gran Corte* to attend to the situation in the spirit of the Prammatiche.

Despite this flurry of activity, his depression about the outcome of the Plan would not go away. At the heart of his state of mind was the fact that he knew what he was trying to do for Sicily was Right and Should be Done, but between him and the king (whom he recognised as king by Divine Right) there was a wall of intrigue built up and maintained by the Sicilian barons who were egoist, obscurantist and destructive, and prevented him and 'poor' Sicily being heard by King Ferdinando. Caracciolo's letters are full of complaints to this effect. Just one example might give some idea of the depth of his feelings: his advice to the king on the proposed candidates for the presidency of the *Giunta di Sicilia*, the key advisory body in Naples for Sicilian affairs much disliked by the government in Palermo for its conservatism. In a letter to Acton dated 23 January 1783, he writes:

The first is Campofranco, the worst of the lot, really dangerous, and if the times were not different, he would be a sort of Catalina. The second is the Prince of Trabia, the oldest, more decorated than the other claimants; and he is an honest man, but he is almost an imbecile and he has suffered a bad accident; his children, who are young, audacious, ambitious intriguers, control him as if he were a child; Chignones, who is well known to Your Excellency, and who is apparently is a position of great influence as regards the choice of the Presidency, became extremely rich to the detriment of the public and the Senate when Trabia was Praetor of Palermo. Vah! *Malam rem* (a bad state of affairs). The third is the Duke of Musulmeri, the uncle of [the Prince of] Cattolica, one time friar now Abbot, is a serious knave, swindler, deceiver and liar to the highest degree; they tell me he is heavily backed there. If he gets his way, not only will we be troubled here, but grave damage will be done to the service of the King, since he is a great supporter of the Baronage and much influenced by the principles of independence, but he will also disturb the Court and Ministers for his spirit of party and cabal, with which he is marvellously equipped.[33]

The Sicilian cabal, then, was still patiently at work, and Caracciolo felt there was little more that he could do, except perhaps follow the example of his friends Turgot and Necker, 'two great men of finance', who had always found it useful to publish what they were trying to get across. So he decided to publish once again Simonetti's *Consulte* and the *Voto*, which he considered to be 'evangelical truth' because

> this publicity for the Plan and this general notion on the undertaking, if now because of a bad star it remains useless, it may in the future bear fruit, fermenting in the mind of the Sicilian People and producing the necessary Reform.[34]

Meanwhile, his health was giving away; the old complaint that troubled his feet was getting worse and he was having problems with his stomach. Such was his condition that he was forced to ask for the king's 'clemency' in May for two months leave to take the cure in the mud baths on the island of Ischia, so he was in a sufficiently depressed mood and painful state of body that when the inevitably fatal decision of the *Suprema Giunta di Finanza* on the Plan came through it caused him no further pain.

The vote of the six wise men appointed by the king to advise him on the controversy was evenly split[35]: apparently, Acton and De Marco (both secretaries of state, and Neapolitan) and Simonetti were for Caracciolo, while Sambuca (also a secretary of state, and a Sicilian) with two other Sicilian ministers were against his proposals. The king was therefore put upon to give his royal casting vote.

The decree was a classic of indecision. The project of a proper land census was rejected, but the necessity of carrying out some form of survey of ownership was recognised; it found that the taxes that the crown lands were asked to pay were unjust, but no decision was offered on how to avoid the injustice. It also stated that the ecclesiastics had to contribute a more just proportion, but made no reference to feudal exemptions. In a letter to Acton on 17 June 1784,[36] which began by asking him humbly to thank the king for sending a ship to take him to Ischia, Caracciolo is surprisingly restrained in his comments about the decree. He limits himself to asking how can the just proportion be found for the crown lands or the ecclesiastics without a census, and what is the privilege that justifies the barons, 'who possess two-thirds of Sicily', in refusing a survey of their lands. A sad man, he sailed for Ischia on 24 June.

11

Picking Up

A fter two months of the mud baths at Ischia, Marquis
Caracciolo sailed back to Sicily on 22 November 1784.
Villafranca wrote in his dairy that his viceroyalty was
'scandalously' and only out of 'merciful benevolence' confirmed
for another three years, but Di Blasi was certainly nearer the
mark when he wrote:

> [W]ith his return the barons began to tremble again, as they
> knew how the feudal abuses were odious at that time and how
> firm and obstinate Caracciolo was in combating them.[1]

In the manner of his return, he sent out the usual signals. He
refused to participate in the gala cortège the nobility had
graciously organised to accompany him into the city, preferring
a private entry, and he later refused the 'pretorian coach' that the
senate normally sent to conduct the viceroy to the cathedral for
the swearing-in ceremony, again preferring his almost private
two-wheeled carriage. All this was deeply resented by the barons
and carefully noted by Villabianca in his diary.[2]

Caracciolo's legs were still giving him some trouble, but the mud
had done his energy levels some good, and he returned with a
burning desire to resume the attack on the jurisdictional powers of
the barons in favour of justice and the liberty of the people. If

anything, the times had matured somewhat. From the early months of that year there had been a growing stream of documentary protest from various townships – from captains of justice, *giurati*, mayors – expressing the needs and hopes of their populations for a better life, some even praising the viceroy for his anti-feudal policy[3]. Even on the intellectual front there was some movement. The Prince of Pantelleria, Francesco Requesens, felt that the lack of rural population was the major agricultural handicap and, publishing anonymously in 1784, proposed what he thought a less radical reform programme than the viceroy's, based of colonisation of the countryside, which, he thought, would distribute property better and get rid of mendicancy and vagabondage. Another anonymous writer of the time thought the agricultural problem could be solved by the institution of agricultural colleges spread throughout the kingdom, which would result in the increase of the population and the wealth of the state. There also appeared in 1785 the *Disertazione Politica* by Giuseppe Costanzo, proposing the abolition of the feudal system and the establishment of a land tax; this was based on many of Caracciolo's favourite teachers (Puffendorf and Genovesi, to mention just two) and very close to his own policies. Not everyone, of course, was avidly reading these books,[4] but some awareness of the problem at an intellectual level had been created, presumably due to the viceroy's activities. And at the other end of the scale there was the beginning of public protest, presumably for the same reason. Caracciolo would have continued his efforts without either, of course.

It is also to be noted that from now his actions were usually initiated independently of the central government in Naples, suggesting that he had learnt certain lessons concerning the influence of the Sicilian cabal in Naples and the inertia of the king. He tended to act first and explain later on many future occasions.

Caracciolo's immediate problem upon his return was the shortage of grain, always a major potential crisis in Sicily, which, because it had the makings of a political disaster, called for decisive action and also brought into high relief the principles behind his public policy. He was overwhelmed with recourses, petitions and pleas from all and sundry about the lack of grain, the price of bread, the increasing hunger and hardship,[5] and he was beset with the memories of 1764, when he had been involved in trying to save such a situation from London. Most people at the time, and many people later, thought that the shortage had been brought about by the freedom of exports, which the Archbishop of Palermo had granted while standing in for Caracciolo during his absence in Ischia; the fact was that the archbishop had granted the freedom of export only a few days before Caracciolo's return and the main reason for the dearth was a very bad harvest, locusts and rain just at harvest time, accompanied by a surge in grain commerce, all of which had preoccupied the government *ad interim*. When Caracciolo got back from Ischia he reported to Acton that he had found the stock of grain had fallen to from 130,000 to 102,000 *salme* in the granaries of Palermo since June and this amount fell to 86,000 a few weeks later; he also heard of shortages in the provinces. He immediately ordered a ban on all export of grain. The baronial lobby had the order revoked in Naples, but he wrote on 12 December 1784 to Acton refusing to accept, explaining that the island had resources enough to live for six months: 'I have not prohibited the export of corn, I have prevented it. *Salus Populi est summus lex!* If they wish to kill Sicily by famine, by God I swear it will not be by my hand ...'[6]

These were the days of controversy between physiocrats and mercantilists, as has already been noted with the publication of Galiani's book: Caracciolo was concerned intellectually with the subject (he was to publish his own book *Riflessioni su L'Economia e L'Estrazione de' Frumenti della Sicilia* later on in 1785) as well as morally and politically, so it was natural that he wanted to control the situation personally. By early training he was a mercantalist, with the teachings of Genovesi, and, though he was open to the developments of economic thought as the century developed, it seems fair to say that he was more influenced by the moral teachings of the French *philosophes* than the pure free trade theory that was gaining ground as the century proceeded.[7] What is clear is that he would not allow free trade if it made the poor suffer. He was neither a pure mercantalist nor a *laissez-fairer*, but a believer in benign state control when necessary in the interests of a fair price of bread for the people, and he imposed this policy without reference to Naples, which was informed later. He stopped exports and instituted a policy of opening and closing the granaries in a controlled way so that speculation of prices could be avoided and the situation could be kept under control. This was far from being appreciated by the barons, who had an interest in manipulating the markets. They made their usual moves in Naples, and this is the reply that Acton received from Caracciolo in a letter dated 2 December 1784:

From a despatch received via the *Suprema Giunta delle Finanze*, written by the Director D. Nicola Nespoli, I see that my project for observing a fixed rule for the grain trade has been disapproved, and since this rule was fixed to open and close at a certain terminal date it in no way detracts from good faith. It displeases me that the opinion of certain people now prevails, people who are not disinterested and who are at present owners of large quantities of grain stored in the granaries; however in the present circumstances what cannot be done by reason has to be done by force, because I have suspended the trade in grain, and Your Excellency will be able to read my reasoning in the Representation that I have sent to the above mentioned Director of the *Giunta*. The Kingdom was entrusted by the King to me, and I shall answer for it, and

> I do not wish to take it again towards the catastrophic famine
> that occurred in 1764; if for private reasons there are people
> who want to risk such a terrible calamity in Sicily, since the
> risk is there, I shall make public the councils I have given the
> King on the subject.[8]

He had every intention of keeping on top of the grain situation as it progressed over the winter and up until the next harvest, and in fact he was able to do so, though the situation was to prove complex.

Caracciolo's objectives in the field of baronial jurisdiction, in the meantime, were quite clear and were converted into a series of despatches and bands that did much to damage the illegitimate feudal power in the realms of local administration, even though energetic attempts were obviously made to get round them as soon as they were issued. He began practically as soon as he landed from Ischia. As early as 2 December 1784 he issued a band abolishing the practice of some barons, who

> unaware of the laws and the limits of their authorities were
> accustomed to issue letters to their local captains ordering
> imprisonments and other penalties on the basis of the phrase
> *for reasons well viewed by us.*

The band ordered all officials on baronial lands to ignore orders from the baron 'in all matters concerning affairs of both civil and criminal justice'.[9] Another earlier decree of Philip III, which was not being respected, was also re-promulgated: no baron or any of his relatives right up to the fourth degree or any of their dependents were allowed to farm the administration of feudal townships, and no sort of direct or indirect interference was to be allowed in any of these townships' financial administration, including the revision of the budgets, which devolved on the *Tribunale del Real Patrimonio.*[10]

He also re-issued, presumably because little attention was being paid to them, two previous dispositions – the annual renewal of all temporary magistrates with the obligatory *sindacato* review (hearing of complaints by a senior magistrate) and the necessity of having three candidates to choose from for the election of municipal officers.[11] These measures were taken because Caracciolo knew both that the barons were diverting money from the royal coffers (his letters to Acton were full of references, both specific and in terms of policy) and the peasants were suffering injustices (there were increasing numbers of protests against baronial injustices being forwarded to the viceroy from priests and mayors[12]). On 10 January 1785 a royal despatch restored election of officials (the *giurati* and the other municipal magistrates) by public ballot to baronial townships, which in some cases caused the existing baronial officials to be seen off by the populace.[13] On 5 March 1785 a further despatch was issued, setting out detailed norms for the annual municipal elections of mayors, captains and judges (civil, criminal and appeal), ecclesiastics and relatives of the baron being specifically excluded. A secret ballot was used, but the successful candidate had to be passed by the viceregal offices.[14] The *Gran Corte* was ordered to request the judges of the baronial and demesnial townships to report every week on the level of crime in their courts,[15] though there is no evidence that they did so. What was achieved with some *éclat* was the destruction of some of the miserable, secret, underground prisons that were part of the feudal justice system and the building of some more humane and hygienic ones. These measures certainly shook the baronial class and raised some hopes in other sectors of society, but did not change the situation radically: as early as 9 May 1785 Caracciolo had to re-issue his *circolare* on the election of municipal officials because he judged that many ballot results were badly carried out or had been rigged.[16] The baronial ancestral armour was, however, somewhat dented.

A clamorous shortfall discovered by chance at the *Monte di Pietà* bank at Palermo in 1785 gave Caracciolo the opportunity to clean up that institute and turn his hand to more general reforms in the financial sphere. The immediate deficit at the Monte was 22,000 ounces, but the final amount was likely to be much more: he incarcerated the governor in the castle, and, though the chief cashier and the accountant managed to escape, this quick intervention did avoid the total bankruptcy of the institution. He felt that 'since bankruptcies were too frequent in public institutions, specially in those left in too many hands' there should be formed a

> Reviewing Committee under *his* immediate presidency ... so that it should examine everything that pertained to the above-mentioned public works ... to eliminate all disorder and to review individually the incoming and outgoing accounts for each of them.[17]

Caracciolo wrote to Acton that he had been assured this committee would come up with some very interesting results.[18] Caracciolo often intervened on the side of financial rectitude in the banks, the bad management of which caused great hardship to lower middle classes on many occasions.[19] He also imposed on every public institution a superintendent chosen from the body of the lawyers, to whom all the administrators of the institutions, who were generally nobles, had to answer. This went down very badly. As Villabianca put it in his diary: 'If our fathers were to come back to life, on the instant they would fight to leave again.'[20]

Although Caracciolo had dealt with his critics at Naples, he had not yet finished with the grain crisis. As 1785 began the price of corn rose and the threat of famine loomed – it should not be forgotten that bread was the origin of almost all social unrest and the next harvest would be in June. Petitions were coming into Palermo from all over the island and Caracciolo made a series of provisions to deal with the situation as it developed. He indicated to the various municipalities which granaries they were to provision themselves from; he disposed that in the more populous cities there should be two chosen supervisors who – to avoid disturbances between the *giurati* for the sale of bread, to eliminate bad judgement, fraud, and to make sure that all went harmoniously – were to be charged with consigning daily to the bakers dough equivalent to the amount of grain that had been administered and to leave the sale of the bread to the bakers. As far as Palermo was concerned, where the production of bread was almost in excess, he put guards on the city gates so that bread and biscuits could not be taken out in quantity thus leaving the city without.[21]

Despite his energy in dealing with the situation, Caracciolo's critics continued to snipe at him in Naples. He refused to open the granaries for export and kept the government constantly informed of the levels of supply in all the granaries on the island, revealing a situation that would not permit of an alternative policy. He railed against speculators in his correspondence, but whatever he managed to do was not enough: people began putting on penitential clothes and going about in procession. Word got about that there was plenty of bread in Palermo and people came from all around, to such an extent that bakeries had to be set up outside the city and extra guards were put on all the city gates. People even began eating leaves, herbs and the blood of slaughtered animals and there was unrest in various towns around the island;[22] two grain ships that had put into Messina because of a storm were taken and forcibly unloaded, as had happened to another two at the port of Milazzo, while Acton on his own initiative had sent a ship full of grain to Palermo at the beginning of May, at which time Caracciolo was informing the government that 'the royal granaries are already empty, something which has never happened in the memory of man.'[23] That year, however, the harvest was excellent and tragedy was averted just in time.

In the joy that followed, the firmness and hard work of Caracciolo was generally recognised, even by Villabianca, who wrote that during the festive thanksgiving 'the praises of the present viceroy Caracciolo were sung since, because of his foresight not less than his firmness ... it did not come about that the Kingdom suffered havoc.'[24]

Having got over the immediate crisis, Caracciolo took what precautions he could to make sure that this did not happen again. Despite the return of plenty, he issued a series of *circolari* on 4 July 1785 that regulated the price of grain and insisted on allowing exports to resume immediately rather than in September, as had been established, so that the kingdom could receive quantities of foreign income, for he saw 'much need of money after this past calamity'. He was also very anxious to quash a complicated grain speculation that was going on, a sort of *bourse* where the commodity was changing hands without the sellers possessing it or the buyers having the money to buy it, which resulted in it receiving a 'capricious price' and a great deal of damage being done. In a minute dated 4 August 1785 he proposed to Naples that all affairs connected with the grain trade should once again be in the competence of the *consultore*, in whose hands it had been before a royal despatch in 1779 had removed it to the *Gran Corte*. Caracciolo thought this would be better all round, as the *consultore* was an impartial outsider, no trader and an eminent member of government.[25]

The 'past calamity' was also an excuse for the publication of his book. Its full title was *Riflessioni su L'Economia e L'Estrazione de'Frumenti della Sicilia Fatte In Occasione della Carestia dell'Indizione Terza 1784 e 1785*. It dealt with the economics and management of the Sicilian corn trade and was published at Palermo, at the Stamperia Reale, in 1785. This was not an earth-shattering treatise, but was an interesting defence of his dealing with the crisis. In essence, Caracciolo did not want the grain trade to be closed tight or left wide open, but somewhere in between, with government as a wise arbiter in the interests of the people. He felt that free trade could be the norm until government had to intervene, a policy that was anathema to the free trade policy of the physiocrats (not to mention the barons). Interestingly, he also disagreed with physiocrats that market forces would make salaries adjust to inflation, and lay down some principles of good government, most of which implied that the monarchy had a duty to look after the weak. His was a civilised book.

Although it has been noted elsewhere that Caracciolo's ecclesiastical policy was relatively mild, there were still some reforms of an administrative and anti-feudal nature he had yet to make. On 30 December 1784 he issued a *circolare* whereby all legal actions involving ecclesiastics were to be heard before lay judges and courts, so that it was left to the king to judge the legitimacy of the sales contracts and the rental agreements that 'the ecclesiastics were *wont* to'. On 4 March 1785 another *circolare* forbade absolutely any attempt to bring pressure to bear on lay magistrates to suspend proceedings when there were conflicts of competence between ecclesiastical and lay courts, which conflicts would be decided by the lay judge and the government would decide on appeal. He regulated the election of parish priests in the municipalities, and in Palermo where the mayor had considered it his perquisite. He parried the protests of the clergy against the abolition of church burials, insisting that all indiscriminately be buried in the new cemetery, and prohibited priests doing trade through third parties. Barons were barred in the most absolute terms from having priests as governors or secretaries of the people on their lands, and priests were likewise barred from taking part in the administration of lay public institutions.[26]

Caracciolo had always nurtured a great interest and affection for Messina. He had been upset when, in his absence and against his wishes, it had been made a *Porto Franco*, and he was further disturbed when in April 1785 Naples declared the city and a large hinterland around it completely or almost completely independent of the legal system that depended on the *Gran Corte* at Palermo (they could only appeal at the third instance). He protested to Naples: he saw that this would increase the rivalry of Palermo and Messina, and of Sicilian cities generally, when what was needed was unity and economic growth. Messina needed commerce, not an 'emporium of litigating lawyers', nor an administrative and judicial organisation, which left yet another opening for baronial malpractice.[27]

Protests from the countryside against baronial abuse were coming in apace and finding their way into Caracciolo's hands at Palermo.[28] He needed little encouragement to begin a further round of reforms. On 15 November 1785 he issued a *circolare* that regulated the question of peasants who were in debt to their lord: while the debtor was not allowed to sell elsewhere and the baron could sequestrate, he could not sell anything of the peasants without going to court. The same document laid down that the baron could not prohibit his vassals from seeding and cultivating outside his feudal lands and that this should be a question of common accord; it also stated that the baron's jurisdiction, his *mero e misto impero* power or his faculty to create officials, could not be transferred to third parties (i.e. the baron could rent his land to a *gabellotto*, but not his feudal powers). Another *circolare* directed at public officials banned the administrators of baronial townships from giving up any of their accounts to their barons and ordered the *giurati* not to give any account of the administration of their townships to the baron, governor or any other baronial official, but only to the *Supremo Tribunale*.[29] Caracciolo also introduced three new liberties that loosened the yoke that bound the peasant to their landlords: the right to bake bread in any bakery (not only the baron's), the freedom to press olives in any press of choice, and the right to sell produce at the price and the place that the cultivator wanted. These were freedoms that were traditionally denied by feudal custom. The duty on milling was abolished and an internal customs duty on staple foods was introduced. He also encouraged new forms of agrarian contracts that were designed to encourage new forms of agriculture: *enfiteusis*, a long-term contract at low rent with the obligation of improving the land, and *mezzadria*, which involved no rent but the rendering of half the harvest to the landlord. The *Monte di Pignorazione Frumentaria* at Palermo was also transformed: this was an institution set up by small landowners originally to retard the sale of their grain crops, but had turned into a monopoly that had raised prices artificially. Caracciolo took this in hand and tried to make the body into an institute of agrarian credit. His idea was that it should be used for the peasants so that they could become smallholders and contribute to the economic revival of the island. He also established a royal granary at Palermo so that the supply of flour within the city could be ensured and regulated, and further issued a band that set out the norms for shops and grain contracts, laying down that these had absolutely to be stipulated by one of the 24 public brokers of Palermo and not by any of the notaries of Palermo or of 24 miles around the capital unless one of the public brokers had been involved.[30]

Although Palermo was no Paris, Caracciolo's interest in things cultural found ample place in his viceregal programme. The salons and conversations were lacking, but virgin territory for Caracciolo to put his reason to work in was not, and he set to work with energy. He organised the foundation of elementary schools in the provinces, as well as new scientific institutes, which he tried to provide with the right modern instruments, and often attended experiments in mathematics, physics and the natural sciences. Great tangible encouragement was given to various scholars: the list is long, but one might single out Domenico Giarrizzo in the field of law (*Codex Siculus*), and Francesco Daniele, the historian of Calabria, as well as the two founders of modern Sicilian archaeology, the Princes of Torremuzza and Biscari. Great support was given to the University of Palermo, which was in the process of being established, and that of Catania, which was fledgling (though not all would agree with this view[31]). He called Marc'Antonio Vogli from the University of Bologna to teach ethics and moral philosophy at Palermo and the Abbot Eutichio Barone from the same university to teach natural sciences: he also made attempts to persuade the mathematician Le Grange to come from Paris. The erudite scholar Rosario Gregorio had his full patronage, and Caracciolo showed a particular interest in Arabic studies, going so far as to institute a chair in the faculty at Palermo. Unfortunately, he installed the infamous Abbot Vella as the first incumbent, who became famous for his falsifications of the Codex of San Martino, though Caracciolo was by no means the only one who had been taken in; the fraud was discovered by his protégé Rosario Gregorio, who set about putting Arabic studies back on a firm basis.

A brief glimpse of how at least the more dramatic of the natural sciences was received among some of the upper etchelons of society is given by Villabianca in 1784. On 14 and 15 March the Prince of Pietraperzia, the eldest son and heir of the Prince of Butera, much taken by the recent discovery of Messieurs Montgolfier, organised a reception on the terraces of Palazzo Butera in Palermo, with Caracciolo, Cardinal Branciforte,

Villabianca and all the best society among the guests, to observe two balloons, which the prince had himself constructed out of ox skins, ascend into the sky to the amazement of all present. This successful amateur experiment prompted an official reply organised by the royal reader in natural history and botany, the Abbé Euticchio [*sic*] Barone, a week later, but, alas, the royal rejoinder was a signal failure, much to Villabianca's satisfaction. It appeared that Caracciolo was most interested because a book exists by a certain Le Roy with the Italian title *Relazione fatta all'Accademia delle Scienze sopra la macchina aerostatica inventata da' signori di Montgolfier*, translated into the vulgar Tuscan from the French by, of all people, the Abbé Eustachhio Barone, 'by the will of Viceroy Caracciolo': Stamperia Reale, Palermo, 1784.[32]

The *Deputazione del Regno di Sicilia* had always been a sore point with Caracciolo and he made another attempt at this period, with the next three-yearly *Parlamento* about to meet again, to reform it. In a letter to Acton dated 25 December 1785[33] he wrote once more how unjust the structure was, only barons and not representatives of the three chambers, a structure that had been forced on it by the barons fifty years previously: he proposed a *Deputazione* formed by four members from each chamber; he put forward all his reasons, and warned Acton not to listen to the barons and 'principally not those three or four serpents who live in Naples'. In the meantime, he would not nominate the new deputies until he received the king's decision on the proposed reform, which was 'very useful, very agreeable to the whole Kingdom, very just, necessary'. He waited in vain. The king simply wanted to avoid decisions of this nature.

> The Frigate *Minerva* arrived here on the evening of the 8th and her captain immediately disembarked to deliver to me personally Your Excellency's esteemed letter, in which I

found the sheet in His Majesty's sacred handwriting with the
Royal Command to leave this island for other destiny there
about his Royal Person. I am therefore preparing to depart
without delay.[34]

It was January 1786 and he had had no notice: the king had called
him to be prime minister of the Kingdom of the Two Sicilies.

The question remains, why was Caracciolo removed from
office, even if his next position was apparently more important?
The answer seems to be simpler than that of his initial
appointment as viceroy, though there are different parts to it.

From Caracciolo's point of view, he was old by now. Ill,
isolated, without friends and surrounded by aggressive
ignorance, he had been sending explicit messages to Acton (his
contact with the king) that he was considering giving up the
struggle. He may have been tired because of the reaction he had
stirred up during his attempts at reforming Sicilian society and
certainly at the lack of support he had received in Naples,
specifically from the king, a conservative who preferred sleeping
dogs to woken, as well as his awareness that his tax revenue was
entirely dependent on the traditional Sicilian institutions and
usages. All this must have been reasonably well known.

But from the point of view of Naples there were other factors
than the distress caused to the Sicilian barony. Prime Minister
Sambuca was no longer considered reliable: having gone back on
his previous anti-Spanish stance, he found himself at odds with a
formidable opponent, Maria Carolina, the queen. Caracciolo
may have been a pupil of Tanucci, who had been notoriously
faithful to the crown of Spain, but he himself had amply
demonstrated that he was absolutely loyal to the king in Naples.
He had, furthermore, wide experience and was known and
respected in the higher echelons of European government circles.
After it had been decided that Sambuca had to go, who else could

fill his place except Caracciolo, the only man of international standing in the kingdom? Despite his years, he had shown himself to be an active administrator in Sicily, and, even if in so doing he had created problems for the king, Ferdinand seems to have realised his abilities because he raised no objections to the queen's move to establish Caracciolo as prime minister in Naples and the more docile Caramanico as viceroy in Sicily.

This time, Caracciolo did not, as was his wont, complain and procrastinate before taking up his new appointment. He must have boarded the ship sent for him with some relief.

Part Four

Prime Minister
Andante sostenuto

12

Naples at Last

⚜

Caracciolo's appointment as prime minister was, by the king's express wish, an unusual occurrence as Ferdinand's interests rarely strayed from hunting, eating or ecclesiastical matters. It was part of a long-term plan patiently orchestrated by the queen, with the intimate help of Acton, to finally cut the ties that bound the court of Naples to that of Spain and to navigate it closer to the waters of Vienna, where her family reigned.

The office of prime minister included various portfolios, but the most in evidence, and, incidentally, the one that Acton coveted, was the secretaryship of state for foreign affairs. He wished for this post as well as all his other offices and the queen was more than willing that he should have it, but the king stepped in and, above their heads, appointed Caracciolo, who had served him with such loyalty over the years. This was in place of Sambuca, who had been ably torpedoed by the queen, as she had previously dispatched Tanucci. Not only had Caracciolo proved loyal, but he also had the necessary international experience, and, at a time when the Neapolitan monarchy was particularly close to intellectually progressive movements that had supported both Tanucci's and Sambuca's anticlerical policies, Caracciolo's known opinions were likely to be welcomed by them.

The new international strategy was important for the Kingdom of the Two Sicilies and both the king and the queen were enthusiastic. It must be noted, however, that the king's unusual energy and enthusiasm in imposing Caracciolo as foreign as well as principal minister did not dispose the queen much in his favour, and Acton, to whom he had poured out his heart when viceroy, was not a little cool. Though nobody talked about it openly, Caracciolo also had another advantage: he was more or less acceptable to the Spanish party, having been the pupil of Tanucci.

Caracciolo himself, though happy to serve his sovereign, had been looking forward to some sort of tranquillity. He was 71 by now (a great contemporary age), and his stomach upsets were not yet cured, his feet still weak, but his mental strength was quite up to scratch: 'Back at home after a long absence, although I desired to find tranquillity and peace', he wrote to Fabbroni.[1] This was not to be, as he was involved in a new struggle 'more exposed than ever to winds and storms'. But the situation was different. With no more battling to change a hostile society radically, he was now more concerned with broader issues of foreign affairs, though troubled occasionally by internal political double-dealing.

As prime minister he was, apart from being foreign minister, secretary of state for the royal household, principal courier and director of the postal system, and also counsellor of state. His salary[2] was 14,395 *ducati* 96 *grani* a year from his various posts (including a retainer as a judge of the Vicaria court, his first, brief unhappy career before being rescued by Fogliani in 1752). He had very little to do as secretary of state for the royal household, as the queen was careful to ensure, but was very active in the other spheres, though the queen put it about – and it was believed, then, and even by some now – that the government was conducted by her and Acton without reference to Caracciolo. That was not the case, as will soon be seen.

He arrived in January 1786 to letters of congratulation from all parts. One of these was from his nephew the Marquis Gallo, whose education he had undertaken from an early age and whom he considered to all intents and purposes as a son. Gallo, who was to play an important role himself in Neapolitan history during the period 1790–1821, had been groomed by his uncle as a diplomat and was at the time ambassador at Turin. Together with his formal letter of congratulation came a longer, handwritten, one dated 8 February 1786[3] in which the nephew poured forth interesting advice, beginning with where he should live in Naples – under no circumstances in his father's house, which, apart from not being well situated for his stomach, legs and digestion, was not convenient for business. On the other hand, he shouldn't live in Caserta or Venafro, which though convenient for business were exposed to terrible weather in winter, and that would involve heroism, 'a virtue that a delightful letter of Your Excellency's once compared to Sodomy and other things outside Nature'. He suggested living in the southern parts of Chiaia and going to court just two or three times a week: this would keep his uncle in better health and make him less liable to be depressed by the intrigues of the court parties: 'I believe it is difficult to find another country more corrupt than ours in this respect.' He went on to describe the dangers in some detail, and even enquires as to how well off his uncle is financially. This was an interesting letter, and it should be noted that Caracciolo did not take up residence in his father's house, but in the district of Chiaia, just as his nephew had recommended.[4] It might also be mentioned that Caracciolo took a reciprocal interest in his nephew's finances: on 11 December 1787 we find him writing later to Gallo in Vienna saying that he had arranged with the queen that his ambassador's salary should be increased so that it would be the same as that of the London ambassador's.[5]

Throughout his time as prime minister Caracciolo had, as his nephew suggested in the letter, to deal with court politics, which meant in particular keeping a keen eye on what Acton and the queen were about. In general, when things were in the open, Caracciolo had no problems about proceeding with his own policies without interference; when Acton was on another tack, or considering one, he acted clandestinely. Two examples at this stage – the cases of Marianna Saffory and the Abate Guerra – might illustrate what he was up against.

Marianna Saffory's case occurred in the second half of 1787.[6] She was the daughter of a London surgeon, and had been packed off, perhaps from Jamaica, to Naples to learn music and the Italian language at the age of ten. She had been entrusted to an English merchant, a certain James Jough, with ample provision, but the girl was not inclined to study and was seduced by certain ladies who induced her to change her religion to Catholicism. Her father's reaction when he heard was to recall her immediately, and so it was arranged, but her ship, the *Betty*, stopped on the way at Marsala to take on wine, at which city she was abducted by her converters and various church authorities and shut up in a convent. A fight then ensued between the consul at Palermo and the viceroy, and the viceroy passed the matter on to the king, who asked Caracciolo's opinion. Meanwhile, Lord Carmarthen in London was asking the Neapolitan ambassador to tell Caracciolo that her father wanted her back, and Sir William Hamilton was doing the same in Naples. Caracciolo simply advised the king that he remembered a case of another English girl in Turin who said she wanted to turn Catholic and they sent her back to England because, if she really wanted to, she could do so there. The king agreed. The girl then tried desperately to appeal again and involved Acton, who pleaded formally with the king and Caracciolo, suggesting even that there would be a public tumult if the girl was sent back, but the prime minister would not change his mind. This was a small incident, but illustrative of Caracciolo's influence with the king on matters that for the king personally were very important.

The case of the abate Carmelo Guerra[7] was based in the court of Turin. The new ambassador at Turin was, from 4 April 1786, the Prince of Marsiconovo; in June the next year he took on as his secretary the abate Guerra, who was strongly recommended by the royal doctor, and in particular by the queen and Acton. The problem was that Guerra's job title was 'secretary' and not 'legation secretary', a change that could only be made by Secretary of State for Foreign Affairs Caracciolo, and which was not forthcoming. Complaints were made – to Acton. Information was collected and passed – to Acton. Guerra asked Acton and the queen also for preferment to other posts, he complained about his ambassador, and he continued passing considerable amounts of sensitive information to Acton, without telling his foreign secretary anything. The ambassador got wind of the correspondence and informed the Sardinian authorities, who opened his post. Guerra found another way of corresponding with Acton. Even Caracciolo found out what was happening in the end. Guerra fled to Florence, involved the grand duke of Tuscany, took advice from Acton, accused the Neapolitan legation secretary at the Tuscan court as 'our mortal enemy', returned to Naples as an accuser and was imprisoned. Acton and the queen, however, got him out, but he eventually left for France. Although Guerra was probably spying on Marsicano (suspected of being of the Spanish party) rather than Caracciolo, the affair does illustrate the ease with which Acton and the queen broke the rules when they wanted to. The fact remains, however, that Guerra left for France.

Foreign affairs took up most of Caracciolo's time and his duties were very varied. There were relatively minor treaties with Turin, always on the lookout for cash: one called the *diritto di Villafranca* gave Neapolitan subjects immunity from customs duties that were applied along the Italian Riviera (the treaty was negotiated by Caracciolo's nephew the Marchese di Gallo in

April 1786) and another (concluded in March 1786) for the reciprocal extradition of deserters and criminals who had committed crimes in one country and taken refuge in the other.[8] There was a treaty with the bey of Tunis that was concluded in the beginning of 1787 and ratified and reconfirmed three years later. Caracciolo also provided arms to the Tunisians and Algerians to guarantee navigation in the Western Mediterranean. Of more substance was the fact that he negotiated from the early months of 1786 a commercial treaty of 39 articles with Catherine the Great of Russia, which was concluded at the beginning of 1787, and which, among other things, opened up the Black Sea to Neapolitan shipping. Catherine had wanted to involve the kingdom in a military treaty against the Ottoman Empire, but Caracciolo had sidestepped the issue. With the prospect of a Russo-Turkish war (it was to break out in the autumn of 1787), although his sympathies were with the western powers, and particularly with the Bourbons, he tried not to get involved – Gallo, then ambassador in Vienna, was sent off to a meeting between Catherine and the Emperor Joseph in the Ukraine in March 1786 with a very tight brief and told to keep his uncle fully informed, but not to commit the government in any way. Catherine asked the Kingdom of the Two Sicilies to look after any eventual refugees (under the terms of the commercial treaty), and both Gallo and the ambassador at St Petersburg urged Naples to consider joining in the treaty against the Turks, but Caracciolo would have none of it, as he explained to his nephew in a long letter of 25 October 1787, even after the Emperor Joseph II entered it in February of the next year.

A major problem in foreign affairs at the time was the state of relations between Spain and Naples.[9] On the one side there was the government of Charles III with its lingering paternalistic interest in Neapolitan affairs and on the other Ferdinand's government with a justifiable desire for independence. What presented a problem for the prime minister was the anti-Spanish party in Naples, especially as this was energetically led by the queen and Acton. While he fully backed the authority of the king of the Two Sicilies against the pretensions of the kings of Spain or France, he did so also against those of the Austrian emperor. His king should be independent of any other sovereign, while still respecting his particular family ties that the queen and Acton were plotting to destroy. The last ranking Spanish ambassador, a certain Las Casas, was spectacularly dismissed from the court in 1785[10] with accusations that he was trying to remove Acton from office and to assert that he was the queen's lover; letters proving this relationship were said to be in the possession of the king of Spain and relations were very strained. So, in the middle of 1786, Caracciolo began a deliberate attempt to soften the tension that had built up between the courts of Madrid and Naples by opening up what became a successful confidential correspondence with the prime minister of Spain, Floridablanca, which did much to help the anti-Acton Spanish party so active in Rome.[11] After Las Casas' departure, Spain was represented by a *chargé d'affaires*, whose invitation to a diplomatic reception in February 1786 was not delivered to him: a small incident, but it was Caracciolo who was apologising to Charles III through their ambassador in Madrid. Caracciolo was also working to balance the hysteria of the anti-Spanish party among the senior members of the Bourbon family. In an intricate manoeuvre, he sought to use the good offices of the king of France to patch up affairs between Charles III of Spain and his son Ferdinand: he chose as a go-between, unfortunately, a French colonel in the Neapolitan army (and so a subordinate of Acton's) rather than the ambassador in Paris (who would have answered to him). The plan also was complicated: Ferdinand was to say he was prepared to jettison Acton in order to appease his father; his father was to answer that he had nothing against the worthy minister. The letter was written, the French government forwarded it, but it never arrived. Rumours abounded, even that the Spanish were reconsidering the question of the royal succession. However, by mutual consent, that line of negotiation was not pursued any further, and Caracciolo returned to his patient work of patching up relations inasmuch as the queen would allow him.

One such complication was Princess di Jaci, who was suspected of possessing letters that compromised the queen with Acton: she had been banned from leaving the country despite her importance, age and the fact that she was a lady-in-waiting at the court of Spain. When she tried to escape clandestinely, it took a protest from Prime Minister Floridablanca to Prime Minister Caracciolo to get her out of the prison into which she had been thrust for her attempt. There were other incidents of a similar nature that needed sorting out occasionally, but in November 1788 Charles III died and was succeeded by his son Charles IV, King Ferdinand's brother. The brothers corresponded, though their queens did not. Much of their good relations were due to their able prime ministers.

The office of secretary of state for the royal household involved the direction of national culture and instruction, a field in which Caracciolo had very clear ideas, experience and much energy. He opened the country up to foreign books, especially French ones, and it is interesting to note the breadth of his interests during this period. We have noted his interest in books during the abolition of the Inquisition already and just before his arrival in Naples we have seen how he had the Montgolfiers' book on balloons translated from the French in Palermo. Two years later, he is writing to Caramanico, his successor in Palermo, from Naples asking him to give every assistance to Canon de Gregorio, who was publishing a translation, with notes, of an Egyptian Arab history of Sicily that the librarian at the Royal Library at

Paris had given him, adding that de Gregorio had nothing to do with Vella and his San Martino Codex (although he was already very scathing of Vella, he did not seem to be aware as yet that the man was a fraud).[12]

A great many new schools were instituted both in Naples and in the provinces and Caracciolo even created a school for the deaf and dumb in the capital.[13] He found the University of Naples relatively flourishing when he arrived back in Naples as a result of the attention it had received from the king and Sambuca, but he felt that it could do with further reform, and got in touch with his long-time friend Fabbroni, who was then rector of the University of Pisa, to ask him for a copy of the statutes of his university with a view to applying them to Naples. The study of the reforms was begun, but nothing came of this at the time, because of personnel changes in the university.[14] Caracciolo was, however, much more successful in his intervention at the Archaeological Academy at Heracleum, which had fallen into serious decay: he reorganised the whole and called in new qualified personnel in May 1787.[15]

Another of his offices, that of secretary of state for the postal service, also gave much scope for reforming zeal, as Naples was in a strategic position for East–West communications. The organisation of the postal department was based in Naples, with two foreign offices, one in Rome and the other in Constantinople. The hub of the European system was at Rome, dealing with incoming and outgoing communications, which were collected, sorted and re-directed there. The problem was that the office malfunctioned.[16] Caracciolo's predecessor, Sambuca, because of his suspicions of Acton, had the post of the king, the queen and the Austrian ministers opened. But that was not the only problem: the accounts were in some disarray because of infighting between the director and the distributor, and one of the employees, who was selling starch and face powder on his own account, had erected the royal arms over his shop and was using this as a dodge not to pay rent to his landlord. Caracciolo sent an inspector up to Rome in April of 1787 to sort things out and it did not take him long to discover that, apart from those misdeeds, the accounts were seriously in the red. By May his orders were to 'cut out all the rottenness', an order that took more than a year to carry out, and, indeed, the exact details of how he did it are not very clear. However, 'a complete plan of reform' was eventually put into place.

In parallel, Caracciolo began work on the existing oriental postal system, which had its hub at Constantinople. He wanted to make Naples the best point of distribution for correspondence between the Orient and the rest of Europe, not only for good geographical reasons, but also for contingent military ones, with the Russo–Turkish war already started and Austria poised to join in. He worked out a scheme whereby twice a month couriers would bring the post from Constantinople via Ragusa in Dalmatia to Naples and from there distribute it throughout the cities of Europe, which he announced triumphantly to Gallo on 11 November 1787, was a scheme the king had approved.[17] The scheme did indeed seem to work before some international manoeuvring and possible hanky-panky soured its reputation. Unfortunately, it died as an international service with Caracciolo.

Probably the most difficult task that Caracciolo had to deal with as foreign minister was the question of relations with Rome, a very tricky question given the sometimes violent anti-papal stance of the queen and Acton and the equally anticlerical convictions of the minister in charge of ecclesiastical affairs, De Marco. One must add to this the Spanish party in Rome, and its intrigues in Naples. The main points in the negotiations concerning the proposed new concordat were the nomination of bishops, the extent of the dependency of the regular clergy on their superiors in Rome, the jurisdiction of the papal nuncio in the granting of monasteries and all sorts of benefices – legal, economic and political issues. At the time Caracciolo came to office the old concordat, which had been negotiated 45 years previously, was a dead letter, and the Vatican had allowed 5 of the 21 archbishoprics to fall vacant, plus 29 of the 110 bishoprics, as well as the office of nuncio (an '*uditore*' stood in for him in Naples temporarily). Despite Caracciolo's own anticlerical background, he managed to conduct the negotiations with Rome throughout on a reasonable basis, steering clear of the sometimes extreme positions of the queen and the devious actions of Acton, making clear distinctions between spiritual needs and political necessities, safeguarding the economic and political interests of the Neapolitan state without damaging the spiritual ones of Rome – receiving, incidentally, consistent backing almost only from the king, a devout Catholic with an interest in ecclesiastical affairs.

His strategy from the beginning was that 'it would not be a question of one side ceding everything,'[18] and that a clear distinction must be made between the Roman Curia (i.e. the church's political entity of Rome) and the Holy See (the spiritual head of Catholicism). This eminently reasonable, or rather unviolent, approach to the negotiations with the Vatican led many of Caracciolo's contemporaries and some of his judges to consider that senility was setting in, but it was more to the point that he had gained much valuable experience in Sicily and was putting it to good use. His objective was to establish the sovereignty of the state without offending the spirituality of the church.

The proposal for a concordat came apparently from Caracciolo[19] in March 1786; his principal negotiating counterparts were Cardinal Ignazio Buoncompagni in Rome and Monsignor Lorenzo Calippi, the special commissioner sent to Naples with a very tight brief. Just three days after Calippi's arrival a decree was issued (28 June 1786), carrying Caracciolo's signature among others, abolishing the dependence of the regular clergy on ecclesiastical authorities resident outside the kingdom. This was, of course, anathema to Rome's negotiating position, so the talks got off to a bad start. During the next 12 months the toing and froing between the sides was constant. Lists of points were drawn up and altered regularly: even the queen and Acton were involved by Buoncompagni and Calippi.[20] By December Caracciolo and Caleppi had 11 articles on which they had reached a general agreement; they were sent to Rome for consideration, during which time the king decided he too might offer alterations (ecclesiastical questions had always interested him) and he did so in his own hand. During the two months this took, the secretary of state for ecclesiastical matters, De Marco, despite a royal prohibition continued to issue aggressively anticlerical edicts. This was not a very auspicious preparation for the meeting that took place on 4 March 1787 at which Caracciolo, and Acton, met Calippi to hand over the articles 'approved by the King' but in a completely new version drafted by the king that Calippi had not seen. To cut a long story short, Calippi took this version to Rome, brought a compromise back, and the situation did not seem to be getting anywhere.

This led Caracciolo, with the king's blessing, to draw up a document–ultimatum on 19 June 1787 under the title 'Project for a treaty between the Holy See and the Kingdom of the Two Sicilies to determine the various controversies and pending questions, and establish a firm and permanent system of concord between the two powers'.[21] There were 22 clauses in all: the first 13 concerned themselves with benefices; 14 (which was divided into 10 sub-clauses) dealt with matters of jurisdiction; 15 (3 sub-clauses) with the constitution of monastic orders shorn of all dependence on their generals in Rome; the remaining clauses were taken up with the prerogatives of the nuncio, the abolition of the right of asylum and other secondary matters. On the question of benefices it was proposed that the king should nominate, for all the bishoprics and all the monasteries of the kingdom, a single worthy candidate for 50 per cent of the vacancies and a choice of three candidates for the other 50 per cent, so His Holiness could create whom he considered most appropriate. He also proposed the election of an unappealable ecclesiastical board of seven native prelates. The scheme was essentially what was practised in other Catholic countries, but it was a wonder that Caracciolo managed to get it through the intransigent anti-Roman atmosphere that prevailed in Naples at the time. He had the king to thank for this, for Ferdinand was involved in the negotiations.

Although the Vatican negotiating party was by no means happy with Caracciolo's document and did not refer the matter to the pope for a 'final resolution', as Caracciolo had asked, they did realise that his document was almost final and, despite threats of breaking off all negotiations, further work of a minor nature was required, which was carried out with the king's knowledge over the summer months. Agreement was reached by all parties, it seemed, and a meeting was called for 19 October 1787 when Calippi was to collect the clauses agreed by the king. On 17 October 1787 Caracciolo wrote to Calippi to invite him to the meeting: on the very same day, unknown to anybody officially, Cardinal Buoncompagni arrived in Naples for 'health reasons' and stayed until 4 November 1787, during which time in a series of secret meetings with Minister Acton he was not only briefed about the situation, but carefully assured by both the minister and the queen that, though the king could be stubborn, he would in this case certainly be open to better terms if the Vatican held out for them. This provoked completely new treaty proposals from Rome, which the king was eventually quite unable to accept.[22]

Needless to say, Caracciolo knew nothing of this, and the whole carefully constructed diplomatic castle came tumbling down. For a long time he was unaware that the new Vatican proposal had even been made and had to write to Rome for news before Acton of all people wrote to Buoncompagni 3 December 1787 to say that he had delivered the document about a month beforehand.[23] It was discussed with the king, who shared Caracciolo's misgivings, and a heavily amended version of the document was finally handed back to the Vatican negotiator on 5 January 1788 to be conveyed personally to the pope with the message that if his master did not approve it the negotiations would be understood to be at an end.[24] Acton's double dealing had made sure of that.

Caracciolo's other major dealing with the Vatican went off rather more smoothly. This concerned a thirteenth-century feudal obligation that Naples still owed to the Holy See, the annual gift of a white palfrey called the *Chinea* together with the sum of 7,000 gold *scudi* on the anniversary of Charles of Anjou's declaring himself a vassal of the pope and of his tribute for the legitimisation of his conquest of the Kingdom of Naples. The Neapolitans felt this to be humiliating and Tanucci had already seriously thought about and prepared the ground for its abolition. The king was willing to continue with the money but wanted to convert it from a 'homage' into a 'devotional offering', and in May 1788 Caracciolo, very much the instigator, deliberated in the *Consiglio di Stato* that the solemn cavalcade of 28 June should not take place that year, nor should the traditional offering of the palfrey, the *Chinea*.[25] The decision was very popular among all classes, though the pope was not happy, as he was very fond of traditional rites, but Caracciolo also had secondary motives for this move. He hoped to stir up interest again in Rome for the question of the concordat by this further dart against the prerogatives of the church. The anticlerical party was very active at the time: in September and October 1788 the regular clergy in the kingdom were declared independent of foreign generals and superiors, and the bishops were ordered to take over control of neighbouring vacant bishoprics.[26] In fact, in June 1789 the pope did give hints about new negotiations, although they only concerned at that stage the reconfirmation of the 'solemn tribute' of the *Chinea*. Caracciolo's answer, in the king's name, was decisive and final: the 'homage' was no more, but the sum of money would continue and any further discussion would be a waste of time. This answer, which was in the form of a formal letter dated 3 July 1788, was harshly criticised by De Marco, Acton's man, in the presence of the queen, on the grounds that it was not aggressive enough and should not be sent.[27] This is another small example of the king's preference for Caracciolo's advice over Acton's and the queen's, a support that had been lacking while Caracciolo was Viceroy of Sicily.

Despite his full agenda as prime minister in Naples, Sicily did not disappear from Caracciolo's mind. His years on the island had left their mark, and though he had little time he followed Sicily's fortunes with some attention. He was personally involved in the choice of his successor, the Prince of Caramanico, who had succeeded him as ambassador at Paris, and his correspondence with him afterwards is full of support, advice and encouragement. Caramanico at the beginning wrote to Caracciolo to say that the task he had taken on appeared too much for him, but Caracciolo wrote back with practical advice, thoughts about political personages, recommendations of scholars, hopes for the humble classes. He recommended him not to forget about the state granary that he had installed in Palermo, which he considered of vital importance, and the same for the cemetery; he discussed the nomination of judges in detail. He often complained about the failure of the land tax, the *catasto*, but when Caramanico sent in the report on how the *Parlamento* in June 1786 had finally made a unanimous request for a 'numeration by *catasto* to equilibrate the public taxes' he wrote to the viceroy: 'This glory was reserved for Your Excellency: I send you my felicitations with all my heart, and the fact makes me infinitely happy.'[28]

Though it is fair to say that this victory and other legal and administrative advances owed their existence to Caracciolo's groundwork, they proved transitory, as their full implementation was held up and then cancelled by the general European reaction to the disasters of the French Revolution, from which Naples was not immune.

Caracciolo continued to give his successor as viceroy advice about imposing taxes and suggested reforms. Caramanico was urged to root out corruption in the University at Catania and to set it in order. He even offered to intervene on an administrative basis in Naples occasionally, as when he wrote to Caramanico in September 1786: 'When you are dealing with the *Giunta delle Finanze* about the provisioning of meat, I shall try to facilitate the means, because the difficulty of providing for the lack of meat in Sicily is not well known here.'[29]

He intervened with people as well: the *Tribunale del Real Patrimonio* needed reforming and Caracciolo spent time trying, without success, to get Minister De Marco to write to Caramanico on the subject, after which he suggested to the viceroy to write directly to the king and he would start proceedings in council without waiting for the minister.[30] And when the Plan ran into difficulties, as it did in September 1786, he was full of specific advice about people to trust and moves to make so that the general Plan did not get obstructed by less important issues, assuring Caramanico he would do all he could in Naples to make sure things went as smoothly as they could.[31]

That was probably as far as Caracciolo could go as an advisor to Caramanico, but as a legislator he was still active in the interests of the king and the defenceless peasants in Sicily against the overweening barons and ecclesiastics. When he came to Naples as prime minister he was followed almost immediately by his loyal *consultore*, Simonetti, who was indeed made minister of justice of the Two Sicilies. They brought with them their belief that the *ancien regime* had systematically stolen land from the crown as well as exploiting the peasants and a precise agenda for reclaiming ecclesiastical and baronial lands that rightfully belonged to the crown in Sicily. It began with ecclesiastical land. The immense abbey of Magione was constituted as an autonomous royal agricultural estate along the lines of Tanucci's *Giunta Gesuitica* in October 1786 and, on the suggestion of Simonetti, the baronial estates of Prizzi and Palazzo Adriano, in the possession of the prince of Cattolica and the duke of Villarosa respectively, were declared royal property.[32] An attempt was even made to take over the enormous estates of the county of Modica, but this was too much of a legal proposition even for Simonetti, who was, of course, involved. A further attempt at recuperating ecclesiastical lands, in this case those that had been illegally conceded in emphyteusis from the abbey of Magione without royal consent, had to be abandoned as simply impolitic, since it was calculated that they amounted to 150,000–300,000 hectares.

Caracciolo and Simonetti, however, were quite prepared to face any amount of opposition in their attempt to restore the crown's rights to the devolution of feudal estates in the absence of legitimate heirs – in other words, their determination to delegitimise *Volontes* (the presumed baronial right to alienate feudal lands) and *Si Aliquem* (the presumed baronial right to extended inheritance to the sixth-grade collateral). A Prammatica was prepared early in 1786 for a new law (not retroactive) and the stakes were clearly enormous; the gestation proved long and was hotly debated, but after much agonising and even the packing of the court (it is suggested Caracciolo had a hand in this[33]) the Prammatica on Devolution to the Crown was eventually issued (14 November 1788), stating that *Volentes* did not alter the feudal nature of the inheritance, but that for the law to be operative a definitive interpretation of *Si Aliquem* had to be prepared – an interpretation that never materialised. A Pyrrhic victory, but he was fighting till the end.

On the evening of 16 July 1789, at the age of 74, Caracciolo was struck down by apoplexy and died.

Conclusion

❧❦❧

Domenico Caracciolo was loved and hated but, without doubt, he was the best remembered Viceroy of Sicily, though he may now spring to mind for the wrong reasons, for instance, for his politically silly attempt to curtail the *Festa* of Santa Rosalia or his formal abolition of the Inquisition in Sicily.

The cancellation of the Inquisition, which has made its mark on many people's memory, was not his initiative – this was in preparation before he landed on the island, as well as in other parts of Italy under the Austrian empress's control. The way he executed his part of the abolition, the use he made of the funds that were released and his care of the vast collection of books, both legitimate and censured, were typical of Caracciolo's character and ideals, because he was a fully fledged soldier of Enlightenment ... a state of mind ill-suited to a conventional politician at any time. The abolition in Sicily was one of the very few times he obtained official backing from the king, because it was not too controversial.

Opinions about him have been divided.

On the downside, he has been accused of savaging baronial privileges without attempting structural changes in legislation and usage that might have achieved deeper, lasting, beneficial reforms. He is also accused of having failed in his major project to reform the *catasto* and, by doing so, to achieve equitable distribution of taxation. The result would have been both social justice and tangible benefits for the king's exchequer. This Plan was the focus of his whole Sicilian policy, but he did not manage to get it through *Parlamento* in Sicily or past the king in Naples.

In reality, Caracciolo was quite unable to impose structural reforms or force through the *catasto* reform, for evident constitutional reasons. He was the creature of the king in Naples, representing him in Sicily. The island was another kingdom and the fiercely proud possessor of a separate constitution, legal system and usage. To make any significant change in those circumstances, the legislative backing of the king was essential, and that backing was simply not forthcoming from a conservative Ferdinand who wielded less power in Sicily than on the mainland and, anyway, had other less complicated things on his rather limited mind. Enlightened ideas and a burning belief in social justice were simply not enough: King Ferdinand had to be convinced and he had to act within the law. This meant creating more than a fuss among the barons and jeopardising the tax revenue voted by the Sicilian *Parlamento*, and as far as the king was concerned this was not on.

On the positive side, the Sicily Caracciolo left when he was whisked off to be prime minister in Naples was fundamentally different from the Sicily he had encountered when he was unwillingly created viceroy. He had arrived with firmly based ideals and had rushed at his opponents with little tact – *de Marte*, as he expressed it – but he had shaken the island up to the point where even the barons realised they would have to make major concessions (and we can see this happening in the gains made by his successor Caramanico on the *catasto* question and in ecclesiastical land reform), gains that were unthinkable without Caracciolo's belligerent viceregency and indeed without his active support afterwards from his position of prime minister in Naples.

The most important thing that he achieved was the liberation of many peasants from a great deal of barbaric oppression, supplying them with land of their own: he worked energetically to this end and, though a great deal was concerned with the suppression of baronial privileges, his efforts certainly resulted in a better life for the majority of the island's population. Of that he was rightly proud. He also achieved much for the cultural life in Sicily, a policy at the heart of *philosophe* thinking. Although the *Academia* was not founded by him, he dedicated much time and money to it, laying the foundations for its becoming a fully fledged university after he had gone.

Though he was blocked in his attempts to make radical reforms by the constitution of Sicily and the ineptitude of King Ferdinand, he made a truly martial attempt to do it (not least in his final, unsuccessful, attempt at reforming the *Deputazione del Regno di Sicilia*). Some results came later, through his successor as viceroy (and through his own active help from Naples). But these were soon nullified by widespread European reaction to what were seen as the excesses of the French Revolution, which was also expressed in the later government of Sicily. There is no doubt, however, that Caracciolo left his mark.

Caracciolo epitomised the Enlightenment – its ideas, its idealism, its contempt of ignorant opposition and its belief in improving things from above. He was one of the very few *philosphes*, or those close to them (with the exception of emperors and kings), who was given the opportunity to try these ideas out in practice, to pit them against harsh political and social realities. But he was not an emperor or a king, or even a prime minister in a constitutional monarchy. He would have liked to have done better, but he certainly did give his all.

Notes

❧❧❧

CHAPTER 1: BEGINNINGS

1   Isidoro La Lumia, *Domenico Caracciolo: Un Riformatore del Secolo XVIII* (Francesco Lao, Palermo, 1868), p. 6.
2   B. Croce, *Uomini e Cose della Vecchia Italia* (Laterza, Bari, 1927), p. 82.
3   M. Schipa, *Il Regno di Napoli al tempo di Carlo di Borbone* (Napoli, 1904), p. 64, quoted in Francesco Brancato, *Il Caracciolo e il suo Tentativo di Riforme in Sicilia* (Palermo, 1945), reprinted 1995 by the Società Sicilian per la Storia Patria, p. 30.
4   F. Nicolini, 'L'Abate Galiani e il Marchese Caracciolo: Lettere inedite', in *Pegaso: Rassegna di Lettere ed Arti* (Firenze, 1930), vol. 2, part 1, p. 656.

CHAPTER 2: TURIN

1   Francesco Brancato, *Il Caracciolo e il suo Tentativo di Riforme in Sicilia* (Palermo, 1945), reprinted 1995 by the Società Sicilian per la Storia Patria.
2   See his letter to his nephew the Marchese di Gallo after his nomination as envoy extraordinary to the court of Turin, dated 15 July 1782, quoted in M. Schipa, *Nel Regno di Ferdinando IV* (Firenze, 1938), p. 86. The letter wishes him luck in his new post and asks him to thank all his old friends in Turin and find out their latest news. He then gives a reading list: Puffendorf, Grotius, Selden, Cumberland – but above all Puffendorf. Principles of civil rights and rights of man derived not from ancient but from modern authors. He should study all modern history and recent treaties.
3   M. Schipa, *Il Regno di Napoli al tempo di Carlo di Borbone* (Napoli, 1904), p. 506. A letter dated 12 March 1753, quoted also in Brancato, *Il Caracciolo*, pp. 32–3.
4   'Breve racconto di quel che è mia notizia rispetto al Trattato di navigazione e commercio colla Francia', an appendix to F. Diaz, *L'abate Galiani: Consigliere di Commercio estero del Regno di Naploi* in the *Rivista Storica Italiana* anno LXXX, fasc. IV, pp. 902–3. Quoted in Simona Laudani, *Un Ministro Napoletano a Londra* (Salvatore Sciascia Editore, Caltanisetta-Roma, 2000), p. 17, n. 11.
5   Laudani, *Un Ministro*, pp. 19–21.

6 The following three letters are to be found in Bernardo Tanuci, *Epistolario di Bernardo Tanucci*, M.-G. Maiorini (ed.) (Edizioni di storia e letteratura, Naples, 2003).

7 The following five letters are quoted in Benedetto Croce's 'Il Marchese Caracciolo' in *Uomini e Cose della Vecchia Italia* (Laterza, Bari, 1927). Croce sourced them in the State Archives in Naples.

8 Président Charles de Brosses, *Lettres familières ècrites d'Italie en 1739 et 1740* (Paris, 1928). Quoted in Harold Acton, *The Bourbons of Naples 1734–1825* (Faber and Faber, London, 1998), p. 76.

9 Quoted in ibid., p. 105.

10 The history of Pasquale Paoli is long and romantic, involving among many others Voltaire and Rousseau. It was Rousseau who introduced Boswell to Paoli; this resulted in *Journal of a Tour to Corsica*, published in February 1768, which brought the issue to the attention of British society.

11 Quoted in Acton, *The Bourbons*, pp. 96–7.

12 Quoted in ibid., p. 97.

13 Letter from Tanucci to Losada, 15 June 1762, quoted in Laudani, *Un Ministro*, p. 32.

14 *Epistolario di Bernardo Tanucci*, 7 August 1762.

15 Ibid.

16 Laudani, *Un Ministro*, p. 39.

17 Ibid.

18 Ibid., p. 38.

CHAPTER 3: LONDON

1 Letter to Galiani of 8 September 1764 in Fausto Nicolini, 'L'abate Galiani e il Marchese Caracciolo: Lettere inedite' in *Pegaso: Rassegna di Lettere ed Arti* (Firenze, 1930), vol. 2, part 1.

2 Letter to Tanucci, 6 November 1764 in B. Croce, *Uomini e Cose della Vecchia Italia* (Laterza, Bari, 1927), p. 64.

3 Letter to Galiani, 8 August 1764, in Nicolini, 'L'abate Galiani', p. 646.

4 Letter to Galiani, 10 May 1764, in ibid., p. 643.

5 Letter to Galiani, 6 December 1764, in ibid., p. 646.

6 Letter to Galiani, 2 February 1765, in ibid., p. 647.

7 Giacomo Casanova, *The History of My Life*, trans. Willard R. Trask (Harcourt Brace, New York, 1967, 6 vols and Johns Hopkins University Press, Baltimore, 1997, 12 vols). References are to the 12-volume edition.

8 For details of the assessment, see Eugenio Lo Sardo, *Napli e Londra nel XVIII secolo* (Jovene Editore, Napoli, 1971), p. 293. There is also a detailed list of the commodities traded in n. 16.

9 T. Smollett, *Travels through France and Italy, Containing Observations on the Character, Customs, Religion, Government, Police, Commerce and Antiquities* (London, 1766), vol. 1, p. 231. Quoted in Simona Laudani, *Un Ministro Napoletano a Londra* (Salvatore Sciascia Editore, Caltanisetta-Roma, 2000), p. 43.

10 Bernardo Tanuci, *Epistolario di Bernardo Tanucci*, M.-G. Maiorini (ed.) (Edizioni di storia e letteratura, Naples, 2003, 13 March 1764.)

11 For the full text of the memoir see Laudani, *Un Ministro*, pp. 101–2.

12 Tanuci, *Epistolari*, 10 July 1764.

13 PRO SP 104/102. Quoted in Laudani, *Un Ministro*, p. 86.

14 Ernesto Pontieri, *Il Marchese Caracciolo Viceré di Sicilia e il Ministro Acton: Lettere sul governo di Sicilia* (Naples, 1932), letter dated 11 March 1784, pp. 191–2.

15 Tanuci, *Epistolari*, 14 February 1764.

16 Ibid., 17 April 1764.

17 Ibid., 21 July 1764.

18 Quoted in Laudani, *Un Ministro*, p. 59.

19 Casanova, *The History of My Life*, vol. 10, chs 1 and 2.

20 I am indebted to an exhaustive account contained in chapter 4 of Laudani, *Un Ministro*. The full text of both memoranda are given in the appendices.

21 Nicolini, 'L'abate Galiani', p. 650, quoted in Laudani, *Un Ministro*, p. 65.

22 Casanova, *The History of My Life*, vol. 10, pp. 270–1.

23 Ibid., pp. 294–5.

24 *Viaggio a Parigi e Londra (1766–1767): Carteggio di Pietro ed Alessandro Verri* (Adelfi Edizioni, Milan, 1980) letter XXXIV, p. 174. In 1766 the publication of the reformist periodical *Il Caffe*, organised principally by Pietro Verri but with contributions by his brother, Beccaria, Pitero Secchi, Paolo Frisi, Giuseppe Visconti etc., had come to an end due to issues of jealousy in connection with the publication of Beccaria's *Dei Delitti e delle Pene*.

25 This correspondence can be found in BA. y. 154 sup. cc 7–31. Also see G. Rutto, *La correspondenza scientifica e letteraria di Paolo Frisi e Domenico Caracciolo* in *Rivista Storica Italiana* anno XCVI, fasc. I.

26 Letter to Galiani in SNSP, MS XXXI. C.13, f. 15.

27 Tanucci, *Epistolario*, 26 February 1765.

28 C.R.D. Miller, *Alfieri: A Biography* (The Bayard Press, Pennsylvania, 1936).

29 'Più che padre in amore nel secondo soggiono ch'io feci in Londra di circa sette mesi, nel quale mi trovai in alcuni frangenti straordinari e scrabrosi.' Alfieri, *Vita scritta di sè stessa* (Edizione critica a cura di Luigi Fasso, Asti, Casa d'Alfieri, 1955), vol. 1, p. 107.

30 Pier Carlo Masini, *Alfieri* (BFS Edizioni, Pisa, 1997) [Biblioteca Franco Serantini]. The book has uncovered two very rare Florentine periodicals of the early 1780s, *Lo Spione italiano* and *Il Corriere europeo*, containing correspondence from a Marquis Licciocara and a Count Rifiela. Alfieri's first biographer, Emilio Bertana, did not believe in their authenticity on the basis of where the letters were postmarked and the fact that Alfieri did declare against Enlightened despotism, whereas some of the letters were in favour of Emperor Joseph II's religious reforms. Alfieri does not mention his involvement in his autobiography but reasonable explanation for this is made by Masini in the book and for Alfieri's anonymity. *Lo Spione* has 20 letters from the marquis and 16 from the count and ran for only three editions in 1782; *Il Corriere*, which ran for 18, has various letters from both, as well as quite fierce criticism of the first volume of Alfieri's *Tragedies*, followed by an announcement of the publication of the second volume, a good

review of it and an editorial apology for having been 'obliged' by an unnamed source to publish the first bad review (a murky business, which may have been a contributing factor to Alfieri's not mentioning these early publications in his *Life*). The published subtitle to his sonnet *Non più scomposto il crine*, dated 28 May 1783 (after, that is, the bad review) and containing the words '*critiche fatte all 1° volume delle sue Tragedie ... da vari Giornalisti ... "Corrieri Europei", e altri simili*', is ample proof that he was aware of *Il Corriere Europeo* and would surely have denounced it, given his character, if it had published letters from Count Rifiela without his consent. The duration of the two's friendship is interesting. The letters, as far as Caracciolo is concerned, are not very revealing, except perhaps for his friendships in Paris and his apparent support for Emperor Joseph's reforms, which was the editorial policy of the publication. Some will be quoted later on.

31 Letter to Galiani, 15 August 1771, quoted in Nicolini, 'L'abate Galiani', p. 657.

CHAPTER 4: PARIS

1 I am particularly indebted to Benedetto Croce's article 'Il Marchese Caracciolo' in *Uomini e Cose della Vecchia Italia* (Laterza, Bari, 1927), pp. 91–4 for the description of Caracciolo's contacts in Paris and their judgements on him.

2 Charles Pougens (printer), *Nouveaux Mélanges extraits des Manuscrits de Mme. Necker* (Paris, 1801), vol. 2, p. 266.

3 Duc de Lévis, *Souvenirs et Portraits* (Paris, 1879), p. 367.

4 J.-F. Marmontel, *Memoires d'un Père* (Stock, Paris, 1943) and Marmontel's *Memoirs* (Paris, 1804), vol. 2, pp. 123–5.

5 Letter Galiani to D'Epinay, 8 February 1777. Quoted in Croce, *Uomini e Cose*, p. 94.

6 Quoted in ibid., p. 93.

7 Dated Paris, 11 April 1782. See Pier Carlo Masini, *Alfieri* (BFS Edizioni, Pisa, 1997), p. 13. There is also a letter in *Lo Spione italiano* (mentioned on p. 44 of Masini's book) by Marquis Licciocara describing 'an interesting dialogue in a barber shop between a Curious Gentleman and a Philosopher about Doctor Benjamin Franklin, the Congress's Ambassador and Plenipotentiary at the Court of France'. Such is the rarity of the publication I have not been able to read the original.

8 This and all the subsequent letters from Caracciolo to Galiani are quoted from F. Nicolini's article 'L'abate Galiani e il Marchese Caracciolo: Lettere inedite' in *Pegaso: Rassegna di Lettere ed Arti* (Firenze, 1930).

9 Letter to Tanucci, Paris, 29 June 1773. Quoted in Croce, *Uomini e Cose*, p. 102.

10 Letter to Tanucci. Quoted in ibid., p. 95. For quotes on aristocrats see ibid., p. 98.

11 Ibid., p. 99. Letter, Paris, 20 September 1771.

12 Simona Laudani, *Un Ministro Napoletano a Londra* (Salvatore Sciascia Editore, Caltanisetta-Roma, 2000), p. 87, n. 6.

13 Francis Steegmuller, *A Woman, a Man and Two Kingdoms* (Secker & Warburg, London, 1992), pp. 76–8.

14 Ibid., p. 119.

15 *Lettere di Bernardo Tanucci a Carlo III di Borbone (1759–1776)* (Registri a cura di Rosa Mincuzzi, Rome, 1969), letter dated 9 June 1772.

16 Ibid., letter dated 5 November 1771.

17 Ibid., letter dated 8 September 1772.

18 Ibid., letter dated 22 September 1772.

19 Ibid., letter dated 22 December 1772.

20 Ibid., letter dated 5 November 1771.

21 Ibid., letter dated 4 February 1772.

22 Ibid., letter dated 11 February 1772.

23 Ibid., 7 December 1771; 31 December 1771.

24 See Nicolini, 'L'abate Galiani', p. 663 (and n. 3).

25 See ibid., p. 663, nn. 4, 5, 6, 7 for references to these gaffes.

26 Ibid., p. 664, n. 1.

27 *Correspondence de Madame du Deffant*, ediz. Lescure II, p. 569. Nicolini, 'L'abate Galiani', p. 664.

28 Steegmuller, *A Woman*, p. 206.

29 Jean François Marmontel, *Memoires d'un Père* (Editions Stock, Paris, 1943), pp. 317–18. '*Sous le feu roi, l'ambassadeur de Naples avait persuade le cour de faire venir d'Italie un hable musicien pour relever le théâtre de l'Opéra français qui, depuis longtemps, menaçait ruine et qu'on soutenait avec peine aux dépens dy trésor public. La nouvelle maitresse, Mme du Barry, avait adopté cette idée; et notre ambassadeur à la cour de Naples, le baron de Breteuil, avait été chargé de negocier l'engagement de Piccinni pour venir s'établir en France, avec deuz mille écus de gratification annuelle, à condition de nous donner des operas français. A peine fut-il arrive que mon ami, l'ambassdeur de Naples, le marquis Caraccioli [sic], vint me le recommander et me prier de faire pour lui, me disait-il, au grand Opéra, ce que j'avais fait pour Grétry au Théatre de l'Opéra-Comique.*' (Grétry, known as the 'French Pergolesi', began a seven-year collaboration with Mormonet with *Le Huron* in 1768.)

30 Letter from D'Epinay to Galiani, 14 January 1777. *Gli Ultimi Anni della Signora d'Epinay. Lettere Inedite all'Abate Galiani* (Laterza, Bari, 1935), p. 198.

30 Letter D'Epinay to Galiani 14 January 1777. D'Epinay, *Gli ultimi anni*, p. 158.

31 *Correspondence secrete*, ediz. Lescure I, p. 312. Quoted in Nicolini, 'L'abate Galiani', p. 665, n. 3.

32 Letter from Celesia to Galiani 31 October 1780, quoted in ibid., p. 666.

33 Francesco Renda, *La Grande Impresa: Domenico Caracciolo Vicerè e Primo Ministro tra Palermo e Napoli* (Sellerio, Palermo, 2010), pp. 36–7.

CHAPTER 5: WHY WAS CARACCIOLO THE CHOICE?

1 Francesco Renda, *Storia della Sicilia* (Sellerio, Palermo, 2003), vol. 2, p. 725.

2 Ibid., p. 736.

3 Ibid., p. 745.

4 F. Renda, *La Grande Impresa: Domenico Caracciolo Vicerè e Primo Ministro tra Palermo e Napoli* (Sellerio, Palermo, 2010), pp. 19–20.

5 Ferdinando Galiani to Madame d'Epinay, 9 June 1781.

CHAPTER 6: WHAT AWAITED HIM

1   F. Nicolini, 'L'abate Galiani e il Marchese Caracciolo: Lettere inedite' in *Pegaso: Rassegna di Lettere ed Arti* (Firenze, 1930), pp. 667–8.

2   Patrick Brydone, FRS, *A Tour through Sicily and Malta*, 2 vols (L. Johnson, London, 1780).

3   Comte De Borch, *Lettres sur la Sicile e sur l'iles de Sicile, de Malthe*, 2 vols (Turin, 1782), p. 5. Quoted in the excellent *Il Caracciolo e il suo Tentativo di Riforme in Sicilia* by Francesco Brancato (Palermo, 1946, reprinted Soc. Siciliana per la Storia Patria, Palermo, 1995), p. 58.

4   Quoted in Brancato, *Il Caracciolo*, p. 58.

5   Ernesto Pontieri's *Il Tramonto del Baronaggio Siciliano* (Sansoni, Firenze, 1933) is a fundamental work on how the Sicilian baronage had become and how it reacted at the hands of Caracciolo's reforms.

6   V. Pettito, *Platea Universale di tutti gli stati, effetti, rendite e giurisdizioni che possiede nel Regno ed isole di Sicilia l'Ecellentissimo Signore Don Diego Aragona Pignatelli, Cortes, e Mendoza. Archivio di Stato di Napoli, Sezione Archivi Privati – Casa Reale, Archivio privato Pignatelli Aragona Cortes, Museo*, vol. 38 (t. II, anno 1734); vol. 39 (t. I, anno 1733). Amply dealt with in Rosella Cancila's *Gli Occhi del Principe* (Viella, Rome, 2007).

7   Pontieri, *Il Tramonto*, pp. 18–19 and n. 1.

8   Carlo De Napoli, *Concordia tra i diritti demaniali e baroniali ...* (Palermo, 1744), quoted Pontieri, *Il Tramonto*, p. 26.

9   Most of what follows on the settlement of the Jesuit land in Sicily is based on Francesco Renda's *Bernardo Tanucci e i Beni dei Gesuiti in Sicilia* (Rome, Edizione di Storia e Letteratura, 1974).

10 Pontieri, *Il Tramonto*, p. 30.

11 Quoted in Ibid., p. 34.

12 Ibid., pp. 38–9.

13 Ibid., pp. 41–2.

14 B. Croce, *Il Marchese Caracciolo* in *Uomini e Cose della Vecchia Italia* (Laterza, Bari, 1927), p. 105, n. 2.

15 Jean Claude Richard de Saint-Non, *Voyage pittoresque de Naples et de Sicile*, vol. 4, part 1, p. 156. Quoted in Pontieri, *Il Tramonto*, p. 55.

16 Pontieri, *Il Tramonto*, p. 61.

17 Ibid., p. 81.

18 G.B. Comandé, *Aspetti riformatori della Sicilia borbonica* (Edizioni D.E.L.F., Palermo, 1957), ch. 3.

19 Ibid.

20 Pontieri, *Il Tramonto*, p. 96. It refers to Brydone, *A Tour through Sicily and Malta*, vol. 2, p. 130.

21 Pontieri, *Il Tramonto*, ch. 7.

22 Ibid., pp. 121–2.

23 Denis Mack Smith, *Storia della Sicilia Medievale e Moderna* (Laterza, Bari, 1970), p. 340.

24 Pontieri, *Il Tramonto*, pp. 133 ff.

25 Isidoro La Lumia, *Domenico Caracciolo: Un riformatore del secolo XVIII* (Palermo, 1868), p. 9.

26 Brancato, *Il Caracciolo*, pp. 67–8.

27 Giovanni Battista Di Blasi, *Storia cronologica de' Vicerè, Luogotenenti e Presidenti del Regno di Sicilia* (Edizione della Regione siciliana, Palermo, 1975), p. 17.

28 This was quite clear to Caracciolo himself when he wrote to Tanucci from Paris about the troubles in Sicily on 30 November 1773: 'The nation [Sicily] has more nerve and vigour, and less good heart than the Neapolitans, and infinitely more union between the nobility and the people; for which reason the sickness must be considered the more serious because the body is more robust.' Quoted in Croce, 'Il Marchese Caracciolo', p. 109, n. 1.

CHAPTER 7: SETTLING IN

1 The *Diari Palermitarani* by Francesco Maria Emmanuele Gaetani Marquis di Villabianca (1720–1802), vol. 18, pp. 165–9. The diaries are included in the monumental *Biblioteca Storica e Letteraria di Sicilia* edited by Giochino di Marzo at the beginning of the 1880s. Villabianca was from a noble family of Spanish origin, passionately interested in history, a diarist and writer who left his writings to Palermo; he served Sicily diligently in a number of non-political offices and revered her traditions. His principal work was his five volume *La Sicilia Nobile*, which was known outside the island, but it has often been said that his diaries (25 volumes covering the period 1743 to 1802) reflect the thinking of the Sicilian nobility of his time.

2 Ernesto Pontieri's *Il Tramonto del Baronaggio Siciliano* (Sansoni, Firenze, 1933), part 2, p. 86 and quoted in Francesco Brancato, *Il Caracciolo e il suo Tentativo di Riforme in Sicilia* (Palermo, 1946, reprinted Soc. Siciliana per la Storia Patria, Palermo, 1995), p. 83. These books, together with Pontieri's *Il Marchese Caracciolo Vicerè di Sicilia e il Ministro Acton: Lettere sul governo di Sicilia* (Naples, 1932), are fundamental reading for Caracciolo's reforms in Sicily.

3 The final despatch was dated 29 January 1782. Brancato, *Il Caracciolo*, p. 85, and n. 19.

4 Villabianca, *Diari Palermitani*, vol. 18, p. 186.

5 Pontieri, *Il Tramonto*, p. 181.

6 Ibid., p. 181, n. 2.

7 Ibid., p.181.

8 F. Nicolini, 'L'abate Galiani e il Marchese Caracciolo: Lettere inedite' in *Pegaso: Rassegna di Lettere ed Arti* (Firenze, 1930). Letter dated 21 December 1781, p. 668.

9 Isidoro La Lumia, *Domenico Caracciolo: Un riformatore del secolo XVIII* (Palermo, 1868), p. 18. See also Villabianca, *Diari Palermitani*, vol. 18, p. 244. The poem is not given in the printed version of the diaries: it can be found on microfilm at the Biblioteca Comunale at Palermo under MCF Q9D103.

10 Pontieri, *Il Marchese Caracciolo*, letter 12 June 1782, p. 71.

11 Villabianca, *Diari Palermitani*, vol. 18, p. 228.

12 This idea of a general market was conceived and attempted as a public service but without any reduction in customs tolls or taxes either royal or private, so it was a failure. See Villabianca, *Diari Palermitani*, vol. 18, p. 320.

13 Pontieri, *Il Tramonto*, pp. 196–7.

14 Brancanto, *Il Caracciolo*, p. 98 and n. 75.

15 Ibid., p. 102.

16 Pontieri, *Il Tramonto*, pp. 209–10.

17 See n. 2, p. 186 in ibid.

18 Villabianca, *Diari Palermitani*, vol. 18, pp. 193–5, quoted in Brancato, *Il Caracciolo*, p. 87. The *circolare* was emitted on 4 December 1781 and is dealt with briefly also in *Il Sogno di un Illuminista* by Pasquale Hamel (La Zisa, Palermo 1995), p. 31.

19 Villabianca, *Diari Palermitani*, vol. 18, pp. 219–20.

20 Ibid., vol. 18, p. 244.

21 Pontieri, *Il Marchese Caracciolo*, p. 73.

22 Pontieri, *Il Tramonto*, p. 182. Letter to Acton dated 27 February 1783.

23 F. Renda, *La Grande Impresa: Domenico Caracciolo Vicerè e Primo Ministro tra Palermo e Napoli* (Sellerio, Palermo, 2010), pp. 52–3.

24 Pontieri, *Il Tramonto*, p. 179 and n. 2.

CHAPTER 8: THE ABOLITION OF THE INQUISITION

1 Pasquale Hamel, *Il Sogno di un Illuminista* (La Zisa, Palermo 1995), p. 45, quoting from Villabianca's *Diari Palermitani*, vol. 18, p. 228.

2 Francesco Brancato, *Il Caracciolo e il suo Tentativo di Riforme in Sicilia* (Palermo, 1946, reprinted Soc. Siciliana per la Storia Patria, Palermo, 1995), p. 92 and nn. 54 and 55.

3 Ibid., p. 92 and n. 57.

4 Ibid., p. 94 and n. 63.

5 Ibid., pp. 94–5 and n. 66.

6 Ernesto Pontieri's *Il Tramonto del Baronaggio Siciliano* (Sansoni, Firenze, 1933), p. 191.

7 Isidoro La Lumia, *Domenico Caracciolo: Un riformatore del secolo XVIII* (Palermo, 1868), p. 18.

8 Ernesto Pontieri, *Il Marchese Caracciolo Vicerè di Sicilia e il Ministro Acton: Lettere sul governo di Sicilia* (Naples, 1932), pp. 75–6.

9 Ibid., p. 75, n. 1.

10 Brancato, *Il Caracciolo*, p. 91 and n. 53.

11 Hamel, *Il Sogno*, p. 75.

12 Brancato, *Il Caracciolo*, p. 96.

13 Biblioteca Communale di Palermo, Qq. G. 96, f. 356 and 357. Quoted in Nicola Cusmano, 'Libri, Biblioteche e Censura: Il Teatino Joseph Sterzinger a Palermo (1774–1821)', *Studi Storici* 1 (2007), pp. 3–4, published by Carocci Editori. This

interesting article is devoted to the work as a librarian of the German Sterzinger, in the favour of the Austrian queen, and of Caracciolo for humanist reasons, mainly at the Biblioteca Regia and sheds interesting light on the acquisition from abroad of censured and heretical books for the libraries of Palermo (many of the unbound volumes arriving in foreign ships at Palermo and Naples packed in straw to save them from the damp). These imports were carried for a long time with the active protection of Caracciolo (even after he had left Palermo for Naples). The article, among many points of interest, also reveals that the last Grand Inquisitor possessed a notable personal collection of censored and heretical (Protestant) books.

14 Villabianca, *Diari Palermitani*, vol. 18, p. 250.
15 Ibid., p. 262.
16 Hamel, *Il Sogno*, p. 82 and n. 13.
17 B. Croce, *Il Marchese Caracciolo* in *Uomini e Cose della Vecchia Italia* (Laterza, Bari, 1927), p. 106 and n. 1.
18 A list of the patrimony is given in Hamel, *Il Sogno*, pp. 79–82.
19 Ibid., p. 78.
20 Pontieri, *Il Tramonto*, p. 211. It must be noted that F. Renda, *La Grande Impresa: Domenico Caracciolo Viceré e Primo Ministro tra Palermo e Napoli* (Sellerio, Palermo, 2010), p. 62 ff. disputes this view strongly and criticises Caracciolo for his lack of support for university institutions in both Palermo and Catania.

CHAPTER 9: CLEARING THE DECKS

1 Francesco Brancato, *Il Caracciolo e il suo Tentativo di Riforme in Sicilia* (Palermo, 1946, reprinted Soc. Siciliana per la Storia Patria, Palermo, 1995), p. 101 notes this and quotes A. Genovesi, *Lezioni di Commercio*, vol. 22, p. 321. It must be noted that F. Renda, *La Grande Impresa: Domenico Caracciolo Viceré e Primo Ministro tra Palermo e Napoli* (Sellerio, Palermo, 2010), p. 77 maintains that the issues involved were learnt at the foot of the physiocrats in France.
2 Brancato, *Il Caracciolo*, p. 96 and n. 68.
3 Ibid., p. 110 and n. 125.
4 Ibid., p. 110.
5 Ibid., p. 110 and n. 126.
6 Ernesto Pontieri, *Il Marchese Caracciolo Viceré di Sicilia e il Ministro Acton: Lettere sul governo di Sicilia* (Naples, 1932), pp. 81 and 85.
7 Ibid., pp. 99–100.
8 Brancato, *Il Caracciolo*, p. 108 and n. 114.
9 Ibid., pp. 103–4.
10 Ibid., p. 104 and n. 104.
11 *Diari Palermitarani* by Francesco Maria Emmanuele Gaetani Marquis di Villabianca (1720–1802), vol. 18, p. 281.
12 Pasquale Hamel, *Il Sogno di un Illuminista* (La Zisa, Palermo 1995), p. 38.
13 See n. 153 on p.116 of Brancato, *Il Caracciolo*.

14 Pontieri, *Il Marchese Caracciolo*, letter to Acton, 28 August 1782, pp. 81–2.

15 Brancato, *Il Caracciolo*, p. 121 and n. 171.

16 Ibid., pp. 129–30 and n. 201.

17 Ernesto Pontieri's *Il Tramonto del Baronaggio Siciliano* (Sansoni, Firenze, 1933), p. 219.

18 Ibid., p. 15.

19 Hamel, *Il Sogno*, p. 53.

20 Brancato, *Il Caracciolo*, p. 126 and n. 191.

21 Ibid., p. 132.

22 Ibid.

23 Villabianca, *Diari Palermitani*, vol. 18, p. 338.

24 Ibid., p. 127 and n. 193.

25 Pontieri, *Il Marchese Caracciolo*, p. 75.

26 See n. 203 in Brancato, *Il Caracciolo*, p. 130.

27 Ibid., pp. 89–90.

28 Pontieri, *Il Marchese Caracciolo*, pp. 103, 106, 110, 100.

CHAPTER 10: BROADSIDE

1 Quoted in Carlo Ruta, *Lettere dalla Sicilia – Domenico Caracciolo* (Edi.bi.si., Palermo, 2004), introduction. Angelo Fabbroni was a longstanding friend of Caracciolo's and at one time Rector of the University of Pisa. His letters to Caracciolo also appear in Benedetto Croce's publication *Una Raccoltina d'autografi* (Traini, 1891).

2 Ernesto Pontieri, *Il Marchese Caracciolo Vicerè di Sicilia e il Ministro Acton: Lettere sul governo di Sicilia* (Naples, 1932), p. 103.

3 Ibid., 13 June 1783, p. 119.

4 F. Renda, *La Grande Impresa: Domenico Caracciolo Vicerè e Primo Ministro tra Palermo e Napoli* (Sellerio, Palermo, 2010), p. 103.

5 *Diari Palermitarani* by Francesco Maria Emmanuele Gaetani Marquis di Villabianca (1720–1802), vol. 18, p. 159.

6 Pontieri, *Il Marchese Caracciolo*, 3 July 1783, p. 127; 10 July 1783, p. 129.

7 Ernesto Pontieri's *Il Tramonto del Baronaggio Siciliano* (Sansoni, Firenze, 1933), p. 251.

8 Villabianca, *Diari Palermitami*, vol. 19, pp. 101–6. He maintains, which is a recurring criticism, that Caracciolo meddles with the traditional ways and seldom obtains anything functional as a result: in this specific case he argues that the viceroy's interference resulted in increased, rather than reduced, costs.

9 Pontieri, *Il Marchese Caracciolo*, 17 July 1783, p. 140 ff.

10 Ibid., 24 July 1783, p. 149.

11 Ibid., 17 September 1783, pp. 157–9.

12 Ibid., 11 September 1783, p. 161.

13 Francesco Brancato, *Il Caracciolo e il suo Tentativo di Riforme in Sicilia* (Palermo, 1946, reprinted Soc. Siciliana per la Storia Patria, Palermo, 1995), p. 151.

14 Ibid., p. 152.
15 Pontieri, *Il Marchese Caracciolo*, p. 169.
16 Ibid., pp. 162–3.
17 Villabianca, *Diari Palermitami*, vol. 19, pp. 62 and 180, quoted in Brancato, *Il Caracciolo*, p. 153.
18 Pontieri, *Il Marchese Caracciolo*, 23 January 1783, p. 96. Quoted in Brancato, *Il Caracciolo*, p. 154.
19 Pontieri, *Il Marchese Caracciolo*, 16 October 1783, pp. 175–6.
20 Archivio di Stato. Palermo. R. Segreteria. *Incartamenti. Busta 3047*, Doc. 27 November 1783. Quoted in Brancato, *Il Caracciolo*, pp. 154–5.
21 Archivio di Stato, Palermo. R. Segreteria. *Incartamenti. Busta 3047*. Royal Despatch 6 December 1783. Brancato, *Il Caracciolo*, p. 155.
22 Pontieri, *Il Marchese Caracciolo*, p. 182.
23 Ibid., p. 205.
24 Brancato, *Il Caracciolo*, p. 155. Copies are to be found in the Biblioteca Comunale at Palermo. Also the undated latter to Acton in Pontiere *Il Marchese Caracciolo*, pp. 181–2.
25 Pontieri, *Il Tramonto*, p. 223.
26 Pontieri, *Il Marchese Caracciolo*, 28 January 1784 and 12 February 1784, pp. 183–8.
27 Villabianca, *Diari Palermitani*, vol. 19, pp. 76–7.
28 Brancato, *Il Caracciolo*, p. 159.
29 Pontieri. *Il Marchese Caracciolo*, 14 February 1784, p. 188.
30 *Circolare* dated 12 June 1783. Brancato, *Il Caracciolo*, p. 159.
31 Pontieri, *Il Marchese Caracciolo*, 14 February 1784, p. 190.
32 Ibid., 2 March 1785, p. 215.
33 Ibid., p. 97.
34 Ibid., undated, p. 182.
35 Villabianca, *Diari Palermitani*, vol. 19, pp. 96–8. Villabianca considered Simonetti a 'sustainer of the project', and therefore biased. He felt that the case was won for the Baronial and so the Sicilian cause, the other side being Neapolitan or not Sicilian and so 'naturally carrying antipathy towards our Sicilian nation'.
36 Pontieri, *Il Marchese Caracciolo*, 17 June 1784, pp. 199–200.

CHAPTER 11: PICKING UP

1 *Diari Palermitarani* by Francesco Maria Emmanuele Gaetani Marquis di Villabianca (1720–1802), vol. 19, p. 323; Di Blasi, *Storia cronologica*, p. 673.
2 Villabianca, *Diari Palermitani*, vol. 19, pp. 232–5.
3 Francesco Brancato, *Il Caracciolo e il suo Tentativo di Riforme in Sicilia* (Palermo, 1946, reprinted Soc. Siciliana per la Storia Patria, Palermo, 1995), p. 163 and nn. 325 and 326.
4 Ibid., p. 165.
5 Ibid., p. 169, n. 347.

6 F. Renda, *La Grande Impresa: Domenico Caracciolo Vicerè e Primo Ministro tra Palermo e Napoli* (Sellerio, Palermo, 2010), pp. 125–6.

7 Franco Catalano, *Il Viceré Caracciolo e La Sicilia alla Fine del Settecento* (Belfagor, anno 7, no. 4, 5, 1952), pp 398–404 for a discussion of physiocrat influence on Caracciolo and an analysis on his *Riflessioni*.

8 Ernesto Pontieri, *Il Marchese Caracciolo Vicerè di Sicilia e il Ministro Acton: Lettere sul governo di Sicilia* (Naples, 1932), pp. 201–2.

9 Brancato, *Il Caracciolo*, p. 171, n. 355 and Pontieri, *Il Tramonto*, p. 274.

10 Ernesto Pontieri, *Il Tramonto del Baronaggio Siciliano* (Sansoni, Firenze, 1933), p. 274.

11 Ibid., p. 273.

12 Ibid., pp. 274–6 details many of these protests at the time.

13 Ibid., p. 276.

14 Ibid., pp. 276–7.

15 Brancato, *Il Caracciolo*, p. 171.

16 Ibid., p. 177.

17 Brancato, *Il Caracciolo*, pp. 171–2 and n. 363.

18 Pontieri, *Il Marchese Caracciolo*, p. 214.

19 Pontieri, *Il Tramonto*, p. 187 and n. 3.

20 Brancato, *Il Caracciolo*, p. 172.

21 Ibid., p. 173.

22 Ibid., p. 176 and nn. 379, 380.

23 Ibid., p. 176.

24 Ibid.

25 Ibid., pp 178–9.

26 References to these anti-clerical measures can be found in ibid., pp. 184–5.

27 Ibid., pp. 185–6.

28 Ibid., p. 187, n. 427.

29 Ibid., pp. 180–81.

30 Ibid., p. 187.

31 See n. 19 in the chapter on the abolition of the Inquisition.

32 Villabianca, *Diari Palermitani*, vol.19, pp. 212–13. There is a copy of Le Roy's book in the Communal Library at Palermo (Pi27, A-D4) and also at BCRS (Antiqua III, 124pp.).

33 Pontieri, *Il Marchese Caracciolo*, p. 228.

34 Ibid., 12 January 1786, p. 230.

CHAPTER 12: NAPLES AT LAST

1 Croce, *Una Raccoltina*, letter 3 December 1786. Quoted in Francesco Brancato, *Il Caracciolo e il suo Tentativo di Riforme in Sicilia* (Palermo, 1946, reprinted Soc. Siciliana per la Storia Patria, Palermo, 1995), p. 195.

2 Schipa, *Nel Regno*, p. 89.

3 Ibid., pp. 90–93.

4   Ibid., p. 93.

5   Ibid., p. 113.

6   Ibid., pp. 105–9.

7   Ibid., pp. 121–7.

8   Ibid., pp. 144–7, 147–8.

9   For the Spanish Question, see ibid., ch. 4, and Acton, *The Bourbons*, ch. 11.

10 Acton, *The Bourbons*, pp. 200–3.

11 Schipa, *Nel Regno*, p. 160 and Brancato, *Il Caracciolo*, p. 200.

12 Domenico Caracciolo letter 9 7/ 1786 in Ruta, *Lettere dalla Sicilia*, pp. 39–40.

13 M. Scipa, *Nel Regno di Ferdinando IV* (Firenze, 1938), p. 135.

14 Ibid., pp. 130–2.

15 Ibid., pp. 132–5.

16 For the postal sytem, ibid., pp. 135–41.

17 Ibid., p. 138.

18 Ibid., p. 206.

19 Ibid., p. 206 and n. 2

20 Ibid., pp. 212–13.

21 All the clauses of the document are given in ibid., pp. 221–5.

22 Ibid., p. 240.

23 Ibid., pp. 239–40.

24 Ibid., p. 240.

25 Ibid., p. 239.

26 Ibid., p. 253.

27 Ibid, pp. 249–50.

28 Ernesto Pontieri, *Il Tramonto del Baronaggio Siciliano* (Sansoni, Firenze, 1933), p. 237. This and other letters to and from Caracciolo and Caramanico are contained in the appendix (pp. 233–47).

29 Brancato, *Il Caracciolo*, p. 205 and n. 46.

30 Ibid., p. 205 and n. 48.

31 Ibid., p. 205 and n. 49.

32 Francesco Renda, *Baroni e riformatori in Sicilia sotto il Ministro Caracciolo (1786–1789)* (La Libra, Messina, 1974), pp. 97–107.

33 Ibid., p. 122.

Bibliography

Acton, Harold, *The Bourbons of Naples* (Faber and Faber, London, 1998).

Balsamo, Paolo, *Memorie segrete sulla istoria moderna del Regno di Sicilia* (Edizioni della Regione siciliana, Palermo, 1969).

Di Blasi, Giovanni Evangelista, *Storia cronologica de' Vicerè, Luogotenenti e Presidenti del Regno di Sicilia* (Edizione della Regione siciliana, Palermo, 1975).

Bonanno, Mauro, *Il rivoluzionario Domenico Caracciolo e il riformismo borbonico in Sicilia 1781–91* (Bonanno Editore, Arcireale, 1997).

Brancato, Francesco, *Caracciolo e il suo tentativo di riforme in Sicilia* (Palermo, 1946, reprinted Soc. Siciliana per la Storia Patria, Palermo, 1995).

Brydone, Patrick, *A Tour through Sicily and Malta* (L. Johnson, London, 1780).

Cancila, Orazio, *Problemi e progetti economici nella Sicilia del riformismo* (Sciascia Editore, Caltanisetta-Roma, 1977).

—— *Baroni e Popolo nella Sicilia del grano* (Palumbo, Palermo, 1983).

Cancila, Rosella, *Gli Occhi del Principe* (Viella, Rome, 2007).

Casanova, Giacomo, *The History of My Life*, trans. Willard R. Trask (Harcourt Brace, New York, 1967, 6 vols and Johns Hopkins University Press, Baltimore, 1997, 12 vols). References are to the 12-volume edition.

Catalano, Franco, *Il Vicrè Caracciolo e la Sicilia alla fine del secolo XVIII* (Belfagor, anno 7, no. 4, 5, 1952).

Comandé, G.B., *Aspetti riformatori della Sicilia borbonica* (Edizioni D.E.L.F., Palermo, 1957).

Croce, Benedetto, *Uomini e Cose della Vecchia Italia* (Laterza, Bari, 1927).

D'Epinay, Mme, *Gli ultimi anni della signora D'Epinay: Lettere inedite all'abate Galiani* (Laterza, Bari, 1933).

Finlay, M.I., *A History of Sicily* (Chatto & Windus, London, 1968).

Finlay, M.I., Mack Smith and Christopher Duggan, *A History of Sicily* (Chatto & Windus, London, 1986).

Hamel, Pasquale, *Il Sogno di un Illuminista* (La Zisa, Palermo, 1995).

La Lumia, Isidoro, *Domenico Caracciolo: Un riformatore del secolo XVIII* (Palermo, 1868).

Lanza di Trabia, Pietro, *Memoria sulla decadenza dell'agricoltura nella Sicilia ed il modo di rimediarvi* (Naples, 1786).

Laudani, Simona, *Un Ministro Napolitano a Londra* (Sciascia Edirore, Caltanisetta-Roma, 2000).

Lo Sardo, Eugenio, *Napli e Londra nel XVIII secolo* (Jovene Editore, Napoli, 1971).

Mack Smith, Denis, *Storia della Sicilia medievale* (Laterza, Bari, 1970).

Majorini, M.-G. *Epistolario di Bernardo Tanucci* (Naples, 2003).

Marmontel, J.-F., *Memoires d'un Père* (Stock, Paris, 1943).

Masini, Pier Carlo, *Alfieri* (BFS Edizioni, Pisa, 1997) [Biblioteca Franco Serantini].

Miller, R.D., *Alfieri: A Biography* (The Bayard Press, Pennsylvania, 1936).

Nicolini, Fausto, 'L'abate Galiani e il Marchese Caracciolo. Lettere inedite' in *Pegaso: Rassegna di Lettere ed Arti* (Firenze, 1930), vol. 2, part 1.

Pitré, Giuseppe, *La vita di Palermo 100 e più anni fà* (Palermo, 1904, re-printed Il Vespro, Palermo, 1977).

Placanica, Augusto, *Michele Torcia e il terremoto del 1783: storia naturale e riformismo politico. Rivista Storica Italiana*Fasc. II, 1983, pp. 419–46.

Pontieri, Ernesto, *Il Marchese Caracciolo Vicerè di Sicilia e il Ministro Acton: Lettere sul governo di Sicilia* (Naples, 1932).

—— *Il tramonto del baronaggio siciliano* (Sansoni, Firenze, 1943).

—— *Il riformismo borbonico nella Sicilia del sette e dell'ottocento* (Perella, Roma, 1945).

Renda, Francesco, *Baroni e riformatori in Sicilia sotto il Ministro Caracciolo (1786–1789)* (La Libra, Messina, 1974).

—— *Bernardo Tanucci e i beni dei Gesuiti in Sicilia* (Edizione di Storia e Letteratura, Rome, 1974).

—— *L'Inquisizione in Sicilia* (Sellerio, Palermo, 1997).

—— *Storia della Sicilia (vol 2)* (Sellerio, Palermo, 2003).

—— *La Grande Impresa: Domenico Caracciolo Vicerè e Primo Ministro tra Palermo e Napoli* (Sellerio, Palermo, 2010).

Ruta, Carlo, *Lettere dalla Sicilia – Domenico Caracciolo* (Edi.bi.si., Palermo, 2004).

Schipa, M., *Il Regno di Napoli al tempo di Carlo di Borbone* (Naples, 1904).

—— *Nel Regno di Ferdinando IV* (Firenze, 1938).

Steegmuller, Francis, *A Woman, a Man and Two Kingdoms* (Secker & Warburg, London, 1992).

Tanucci, Bernardo, *Epistolario di Bernardo Tanucci*, M.-G. Maiorini (ed.) (Edizioni di storia e letteratura, Naples, 2003).

Verri, Pietro and Alessandro, *Viaggio a Parigi e Londra (1766–1767): Carteggio di Pietro e Alessandro Verri* (Edizioni Adelfi, Milano, 1980).

Villabianca, Marquis of, *Diari Palermitani*, published in the monumental *Biblioteca Storica e Letteraria di Sicilia*, Giochino di Marzo (ed.) at the beginning of the 1880s. Vols 18 and 19 cover Caracciolo's time in Palermo.

Index

Abolition of the Inquisition, 115–123

Academia, 94, 95, 123, 205

Acton, Sir John: appointment of Caracciolo as Viceroy, 67–69; baronial privilege, 84, 161–166, 172–173; Caracciolo as prime minister, 185–188, 191–199; Caracciolo as Viceroy, 84, 106, 112–113, 126–128, 132, 134, 140–141, 146–148, 150–155, 157–159, 161–166, 169–170, 172–174, 180–181; correspondence with Caracciolo, 106, 112–113, 118, 127, 128, 132, 134; grain crisis, 169, 170, 174; Messina reconstruction, 146–147, 150–155, 157–158

Agriculture, 7, 15, 34, 35, 81–85, 168, 178

Airoldi, President, 81, 104, 133, 136, 137

Aix-la-Chapelle, Treaty of, 8, 11, 13, 18

Alcantara Porras y Silva, D. Maria de, 3

Alfieri, Count Vittorio, 4, 41–42, 208n.28–30, 209n.7

Alfonso, King, 81, 132

Aprile, Alicia, 128

Archaeological Academy, Heracleum, 193

Aristocracy, 6, 68, 85, 127–128

Army, 6, 97, 104, 116

Austria, 8, 11, 13, 17, 52, 66, 191, 194

Avignon, 50, 55

Azienda Gesuitica, 77, 78

Balducci, Marina, 105–106

Baltimore, Lord, 26

Banks, Sir Joseph, 43

Barbarici, Canon, 122

Barone, Abbot Eutichio, 179, 180

Barons: appointment of Caracciolo as Viceroy, 65, 68; Caracciolo as prime minister, 201; Caracciolo as Viceroy, 103, 105, 110–113, 116, 125, 127–130, 133–135, 150–157, 161–164, 166–168, 171–172, 176–178, 180; Caracciolo legacy, 203–205; what awaited Caracciolo as Viceroy, 72–76, 78–85, 87–92, 94–95, 97

Bedford, Duke of, 38

Bertana, Emilio, 208n.30
Biscari, Prince of, 94, 179
Bishops, 90, 109, 194, 197, 199
Black Sea, 190
Books, 121–122, 159–160, 192,
    203, 213–214n.13
Bourbon family, 125, 190, 191
Brancato, Francesco, 11
Branciforte, Cardinal, 179
Bread prices, 85–86, 87, 95, 105,
    108, 169, 170, 173–174, 178
Breteuil, Baron de, 59
Britain, 26–32, 33–35, 36–38, 52
Brydone, Patrick, 72, 87
Buoncompagni, Cardinal Ignazio,
    195, 196, 197, 198
Burials, 107, 110, 176
Butera family, 163
Butera, Prince of, 90, 179

Calippi, Lorenzo, 195, 196, 197
Camporeale, Prince of, 68
Capitoli, 67, 78, 88
Caracciolo, Domenico: abolition of
    the Inquisition, 115–123; as
    ambassador in London, 20–22,
    23–43; as ambassador in Paris,
    4, 42, 45–60, 103; appointment
    as Viceroy, 60, 63–69; baronial
    privilege, 77, 84–85, 87–88,
    110–111, 134–135, 161–166,
    167–168, 171–172, 176–178;
    birth, 3; books and literature, 4,
    55, 117, 159–160; *catasto* (land
    survey) reform, 14–15, 125,
    129–131, 140–141, 147, 204;
    commerce, 24, 26–32, 52–53,
    128–129; correspondence with
    Acton, 106, 112–113, 118, 127,
    128, 132, 134; correspondence

with Calabritto, 21–22;
correspondence with Fabbroni,
143–146; correspondence with
Fogliani, 12; correspondence
with Galiani, 6–7, 23–25, 35, 38,
41, 43, 48–51, 55–56, 68–69, 71,
106; correspondence with
Tanucci, 8, 14–16, 18–21, 24,
28–29, 31, 33–35, 42, 49;
cultural life, 39–42, 45–47,
93–94, 178–181, 192–194, 205;
death of, 202; as diplomat,
3–60; as diplomat in Turin,
11–22; early life, 3–7;
ecclesiastical reforms, 4, 16–17,
50, 103, 108–109; education and
schooling, 3–5, 7, 193; foreign
affairs, 189–192, 194–202; grain
crisis, 83, 86, 105, 168–171,
173–176; health, 57–58, 60, 165,
167, 186; judicial system, 5–6,
12, 80–81, 104, 107, 110,
126–127, 139, 187–188; legacy,
203–205; *Marmorari* affair,
135–139; Messina tax, 146–157;
monarchism, 48–49, 103;
musical *querelle*, 4, 58–60;
opposition to reforms, 115–119;
personality and physiognomy,
46–47; postal service, 158–159,
193–194; as prime minister,
181, 185–202; private/love life,
3–4, 60, 105–106; relations with
Rome, 194–199; *Riflessioni su
L'Economia e L'Estrazione de'
Frumenti della Sicilia*, 56, 169,
175–176; road reforms, 108,
131, 132; Santa Rosalia *Festa*,
147–148, 152, 153, 203;
Scarnicchia affair, 32–33; silk

trade, 14, 36–38; social justice reforms, 125–128; as Viceroy: broadside, 143–166; as Viceroy: clearing the decks, 125–141; as Viceroy: picking up, 167–182; as Viceroy: settling in, 101–113; as Viceroy: what awaited him, 71–97

Caracciolo, Tommaso, 3

Caramanico, Prince of, 192, 199, 200, 204

Carmarthen, Lord, 188

Carnivals, 108, 109, 113

Carriage tax, 131

Casa di Nostra Signora delle Derelitte, 123

Casanova, Giacomo, 26, 36, 38–39

Cassaro, Prince of, 95–96

Castellamare prison, 136

Castelvetrano, Prince of, 74

Catania, 88, 154, 179, 200

Catasto (land survey), 14–15, 49, 73, 103, 125, 129–131, 140, 143, 146–148, 154, 165–166, 168, 199, 203–204

Catherine the Great, 56, 190

Catholicism, 119, 194–199

Cattolica family, 163

Cattolica, Prince of, 39, 84, 164, 201

Celesia, Pietro Paolo, 57, 60

Cemeteries, 107, 109, 110, 140, 144–145, 158, 176, 199

Charles Emmanuel, King, 17, 18, 19

Charles III, King of Spain, 7, 8, 11, 13, 15, 17, 19, 30–32, 36, 63–67, 79, 92, 190–192

Charles IV, 192

Charles of Anjou, 198

Charlotte, Queen, 36

Chinea, 73, 198–199

Church, 5, 6, 16–17, 74, 88, 103, 108–109, 123, 194–199

Clement IV, Pope, 65

Codex of San Martino, 179, 193

Codex Siculus, 179

Codice di Melfi, 63, 67

Colonna Frumentaria, 86, 95

Colonna, Marcantonio (Prince of Stigliano), 97

Commerce, 26–32, 33–38, 52, 81–85, 128, 132

Commercial treaties, 26–32, 52, 190

Compagnia dei Bianchi, 127–128

Consiglio di Stato, 66, 198

Constantinople, 193, 194

Constitution, 63–64, 72, 78, 87, 88, 205

Constutiones divae memoriae (Frederick II), 75

Cook, Captain James, 43

Corn market, 33–35, 55, 82, 83, 86, 132, 173, 176

Il Corriere europeo, 208–209n.30

Corsairs, 27, 108, 128

Corsica, 18, 19

Corsini, Prince, 112

Corte dei Presidenti e Consulente, 128

Corte di Napoli, 156

Costanzo, Giuseppe, 168

Courts, 6, 79–81, 104, 110, 139, 176

Craftsmen's guilds, 65, 96, 97, 107, 133, 134

Croce, Benedetto, 4

Cultural life, 39–42, 45–47, 93–94, 178–181, 192–194, 205

D'Aiguillon, Duc, 55

D'Alembert, Jean le Rond, 41, 45, 48, 50, 119, 122, 123, 145

Daniele, Francisco, 179

D'Aragon, Marquis, 39
D'Aragona, Prince, 132, 133, 134
De Borch, Comte, 72
De Brosses, Charles, 17
De concessione feudi, 117
Deffant, Madame du, 58
De gravitate universali corporum, 40–41
De Gregorio, Canon, 192–193
De Gregorio, Pietro, 117
De judiciis causarum feudalium, 117
De Marco, Minister, 137, 165, 194, 196, 199, 200
Denti, Bernardino, 115
D'Epinay, Madame, 45, 47, 58, 59, 69
Deputazione del Regno di Sicilia, 67–68, 91, 141, 147, 149, 151, 152, 180, 205
Descrizione, 73
De successione nobelium in feudis (Frederick II), 75
D'Holbach, Baron, 45, 50
Dialogues sur le commerce des blés (*Dialogues on the commerce of corn*), 55, 56
Di Blasi, Francesco Paolo, 93–94
Di Blasi, Giovanni Battista, 94, 167
Diderot, Denis, 48, 56
Didone, 58
Di Jaci, Princess, 192
Di Napoli, Carlo, 76, 117
Diritto di Villafranca, 189
Disertazione Politica (Costanzo), 168
Il Dizionario Bibliografico degli Italiani, 47
D'Olivares, Count, 79
Donativi (gifts), 92, 129, 140, 148–154, 156, 157
Don Philip, 11, 18

D'Orléons, Duc, 57
Drago, Casmiro, 118
Du Barry, Madame, 50, 59

East Indies, 32, 33, 55
Ecclesiastical reforms, 108–109
Ecclesiastics, 14, 49, 92, 130, 147, 149–151, 166, 172, 176, 201
Economics, 23, 81–85
Education, 5, 49, 65, 179, 193
Elections, 126, 162, 172, 176
Emile (Rousseau), 17
Emphyteusis, 77, 78, 81, 82, 201
Enfiteusis, 178
England, 52, 53, 54
Enlightened despotism, 5, 67, 113
Enlightenment, 93, 203, 205
L'Esprit (Helvétius), 51

Fabbroni, Angelo, 143, 186, 193
Famine, 77, 86, 95, 171, 173
Federico II University, 5
Ferdinand, King, 8, 11, 15, 18, 79, 182, 185, 190, 197, 204, 205
Ferdinando, King, 64, 164
Festa of Santa Rosalia, 87, 147–148, 152, 153, 203
Feudal system, 35, 72–76, 80, 88, 90, 93, 168, 171, 176–178, 201–202
Filangieri, Archbishop, 96, 97
Floridablanca, Prime Minister, 191, 192
Fogliani di Aragona, Marquis Giovanni, 7, 11–13, 36, 65, 68, 77, 78, 86–87, 94–97, 107, 116, 186
Food prices, 85–87, 89, 95, 105, 107, 110, 170, 178
France, 30, 32, 37, 38, 52, 52, 53, 191

Frankish tradition, 75

Franklin, Benjamin, 41, 48

Frederick II, 75

Frederick III of Aragon, 75

Free trade, 35, 56, 170, 176

French Opéra, 59

French Revolution, 200, 205

Frisi, Paolo, 40–41

Gabellotti (large tenant farmers), 78, 82–85, 90, 177

Gaffori, François, 19

Galiani, Abbé, 6–7, 23–25, 35, 38, 39, 41, 43, 45–52, 55–60, 68–69, 71, 103, 104, 106, 169

Gallo, Marquis, 12, 186–187, 189, 190, 194, 206n.2

Gargano, Giuseppe, 112, 113, 120, 149, 151, 154, 157

Garibaldi, Giuseppe, 63

Gazzaniga, Giuseppe, 106

Genovesi, Antonio, 5, 6, 8, 35, 64, 65, 77, 125, 168, 170

Geoffrin, Madame, 26, 45, 50

Geraci, Marchioness di, 131

Geraci, Marquis of, 116, 162

Geraci-Ventimiglia family, 161, 162

Giannone, Pietro, 5, 8, 55, 64

Giarrizzo, Domenico, 179

Gimoard, Comte de, 48

Giudice delegato (delegated judge), 27, 32, 33

Giunta di Sicilia, 69, 92, 138, 146, 164

Giurati (locally elected magistrates), 110, 162, 172, 174, 177

Gluck, Christoph Willibald, 4, 58, 59–60

Grain crisis, 26, 33–35, 55–56, 168–171, 173–176, 178

Gran Corte, 78, 104, 110, 111, 115, 126, 160, 161, 163, 172, 175, 177

Gregorio, Rosario, 94, 179

Guerra, Abate Carmelo, 82–83, 188, 189

Guilds, 65, 96, 97, 107, 133, 134

Halifax, Lord, 26, 28, 29, 30, 31, 32, 36

Hamilton, Sir William, 26, 32, 36, 43, 188

Hapsburgs, 13, 52

Harrison, Commodore, 28

Helvétius, Claude Adrien, 45, 48, 50–51

Helvétius, Madame, 51

History of His Life (Casanova), 26

Holland, Lady, 26

Holy See, 195, 196, 198

House of Savoy, 13, 16, 17

Hume, David, 40, 48, 94

In Aliquibis (Frederick II), 75

Inquisition, 93, 111, 119–123, 143, 203

Ischia, 165, 166, 167, 169

Istoria filosofica e politica del commercio e dello stabilimento degli europei nelle due Indie (*Philosophical and political history of the commerce and the establishment of Europeans in the two Indies*), 55

Italian League, 19

Italy, 8, 63, 66, 72, 189

James of Aragon, 75

Jesuits, 65, 67, 77, 94, 95

Joseph, Emperor, 68, 190

Joseph II, Emperor, 190, 208n.30
Jough, James, 188
Journal del Paris, 60
Judges, 6, 126–127, 137, 138, 162, 172, 199
Judicial system, 79–81, 110, 126–127, 139, 172, 176

Kingdom of Italy, 63
Kingdom of the Two Sicilies: appointment of Caracciolo as Viceroy, 64; Caracciolo as ambassador in London, 26, 29, 31, 33–34, 35; Caracciolo as ambassador in Paris, 49, 52–53; Caracciolo as diplomat in Turin, 11, 14, 17, 18; Caracciolo as prime minister, 185, 190, 191, 196; Caracciolo as Viceroy of Sicily, 160, 181; reform of Kingdom, 7

La Grange, Joseph-Louis, 4, 41, 179
Lampedusa, 53–54
Landholding, 65, 73–75, 77–78, 165
Land survey *see catasto*
Las Casas, 191
Latifondi (large feudal estates), 73–74, 81–82, 84
Legal matters, 6, 79–80, 107, 110, 115, 179
Leopold, Emperor, 59
Lespinasse, Mademoiselle, 45, 50, 58
Lettre de M. le Marquis de Caracioli à M. d'Alembert, 47–48
Lévis, Duc de, 46
Libraries, 121–122
Licciocara, Marquis, 48, 208n.30, 209n.7

Liebnitz, Gottfried Wilhelm, 93, 94
Ligonier, Lord, 41, 42
Literature, 4, 117
Lo Castro, Emmanuele, 149, 151, 152–153, 156, 157
Lombard tradition, 75
London, 20, 21–22, 36–38, 169
Lorenzi, Giambattista, 58
Lorenzo Il Magnifico, 145
Losada, Duke of, 20, 21, 39
Louis XV, 3, 18, 48, 49, 56, 59
Louis XVI, 39, 57, 58, 60
Luigi dei Medici, 66

Magistrature, 5, 80, 81, 110, 172, 176
Malta, 53–54
Maria Carolina, Queen, 66, 181
Maria Theresa, Empress, 18, 66, 119, 125, 141, 147
Marie Antoinette, Queen, 57, 58, 59, 66
Marmontel, 46–47, 48, 58–59
Marmorari affair, 135–139, 146
Marsala, 92, 188
Marsiconovo, Prince of, 189
Masques, 108, 109, 113
Masserano, Prince, 42
Maupeou *coup d'état*, 48–49
Memoires (Marmontel), 58–59
Mercantalists, 169–170
Mercure de France, 122
Messina, 93, 118–119, 132, 139, 146–149, 154, 156, 160, 174, 177
Milan, 8, 141, 147
Milanese, Francesco, 117
Milazzo, 135, 174
Modica, 163, 201
Monarchy, 5, 48–49, 73, 75, 88, 90, 103, 176

Mongitore, Antonio, 117
Monks, 49, 109, 195
Monte di Pietà bank, 173
Monte di Pignorazione Frumentaria, 178
Montesquieu, 48, 51
Montgolfier brothers, 179, 180, 192
Mora Pignatelli, Marquis of, 39
Music, 4, 58–60
Musulmeri, Duke of, 164

Naples: appointment of Caracciolo as Viceroy, 63, 64, 65, 68; Caracciolo as ambassador in London, 27, 36; Caracciolo as ambassador in Paris, 56–57; Caracciolo as diplomat in Turin, 12, 14, 17; Caracciolo as prime minister, 185–202; Caracciolo as Viceroy, 128, 129, 131, 132, 146, 156, 160, 168, 177; Caracciolo as Viceroy of Sicily, 71, 72, 73, 103; early life of Caracciolo, 4, 6–7
Naselli, Don Baldassare (Prince d'Aragona), 132
Natale, Tomaso, 93
Natural sciences, 179–180
Necker, Jacques, 47, 48, 165
Necker, Madame, 45
Neri, Pompeo, 141
Nobility, 17, 87–91, 94–95
Norman–Hohenstaufen constitution, 78
Normans, 76, 162
Numerazione, 73
Nuns, 109, 111, 144

Opera, 25, 58–60
Order of San Gennaro, 55
Ottoman Empire, 32, 190

Pagliette, 80
Paisiello, Giovanni, 58
Palazzo brothers, 135–137
Palazzo Steri, 120
Palermo, 8, 32, 63–65, 71–73, 82, 85–88, 92–93, 95–96, 101–103, 128–132, 139–140, 146, 150, 158, 160, 174, 177–178
Palermo, Archbishop of, 90, 94, 109, 120, 169
Palermo, Gaspare, 117
Pantelleria, Prince of, 78, 168
Paoli, Pasquale, 19
Papacy, 5, 50, 105, 109, 194–199
Paris, 4, 12, 20, 45–60, 63, 103
Parlamento, 63, 64, 67, 76–79, 90–92, 105, 109, 125, 129–130, 140, 146–147, 149–151, 153–154, 180, 199, 204
Parma, 11, 18
Parma, Duke of, 11, 63
Paternò family, 89
Paternò, Judge, 77
Peasantry, 75, 77–78, 81–82, 90, 111, 127, 172, 177–178, 201, 205
Pembroke, Lord, 26
Philip III, 171
Philip V of Spain, 11
Philosophes, 45, 93, 123, 170, 205
Physiocrats, 55, 56, 57, 169, 176
Piacenza, 18, 21
Piazza, Giuseppe, 123
Piccinni, Niccolò, 4, 58, 59
Piedmontese silk, 14, 37
Pietraperzia, Prince of, 136, 137, 138, 139, 146, 179, 180
Pignatelli Cortes e Mendoza, Don Diego Aragona, 74
Pignatelli, Prince, 42–43
Piracy, 28, 128

Pitt, Penelope, 41, 42
Pitt, William, 19, 38
Pope, 109, 132, 197, 199
Postal service, 140, 158–159,
 193–194
Praslin, Duke of, 54
Priests, 15, 77, 96, 116, 176, 177
Prisons, 89, 96, 136, 163, 172
Privileges, 88, 92, 132–135, 158,
 161–164, 166
Prussia, 8, 52
Puffendorf, Samuel von, 168, 206n.2

Raynal, Abbé, 55
Real Pubblica Libreria del Senato,
 121, 122
*Regia Accademia degli Studi di
 Palermo*, 123
*Relazione fatta all'Accademia delle
 Scienze sopra la macchina
 aerostatica inventata da' signori
 di Montgolfier*, 180
Religion, 49, 108–109, 127–128,
 194–199
Requesens, Francesco, 168
Rifiela, Count, 208n.30
*Riflessioni su L'Economia e
 L'Estrazione de' Frumenti della
 Sicilia* (Caracciolo), 56, 169,
 175–176
Right to carry arms, 132, 133–134
Riots, 33, 78, 85, 86, 96, 107, 133
Road reforms, 108, 131, 132, 158
Roger, Great Count, 76, 162
Roger II, 75
Roland, 59, 60
Roman Curia, 49, 195
Rome, 8, 193, 194–199
Rousseau, Jean-Jacques, 17, 40, 48,
 93

Royal Society, 40, 41
Russia, 8, 52, 83, 190
Russo–Turkish war, 190, 194

Saffory, Marianna, 188
Saint-Non, Jean Claude Richard de,
 82
Saint-Vast, Madame de, 25–26
Salons, 45–47
Sambuca, Marquis of, 66–69, 78,
 95, 101, 116, 119, 147, 157–158,
 165, 181, 185, 193
Sandwich, Lord, 31
San Martino Codex, 179, 193
Sannicando, Prince of, 65
Santa Croce, Marquis di, 107, 135,
 136
Santa Rosalia *Festa*, 87, 147–148,
 152, 153, 203
San Teodoro, Duke of, 7
Santo Lucido, Marchese di, 41
Sant'Uffizio (the Inquisition), 93,
 111, 119–123, 143, 203
Sardinia, 8, 11, 13, 14, 19, 20
Savoy, 8, 13, 16, 17
Scarnicchia, Captain, 32–33
Schooling, 65, 109, 110, 179, 193
Sciences, 179–180
Scire, 75
Sculpture, 117–118
Seven Years' War, 8, 17, 19
Ship inspections, 27–32
Si Aliquam, 75, 76, 78, 201, 202
Sicily: abolition of the Inquisition,
 115–123; appointment of
 Caracciolo as Viceroy, 63–69;
 Caracciolo as ambassador in
 London, 28, 33, 36–37;
 Caracciolo as diplomat in Turin,
 17; Caracciolo as prime minister,

199–201; Caracciolo as Viceroy, 125, 129–132, 140–141, 146, 151–152, 157, 160–162, 165–166, 168–171; Caracciolo legacy, 203–205; Caracciolo settling in as Viceroy, 101–113; Genovesi and Giannone teachings, 5; reform of Kingdom, 7, 8–9; what awaited Caracciolo as Viceroy, 71–97 *see also* Kingdom of the Two Sicilies

Silesia, 8, 11

Silk trade, 14, 26, 36–37, 83

Simonetti, Saverio, 112, 113, 119–122, 129, 140–141, 146, 150, 154, 156–158, 165, 201

Sindacato (inspection), 89, 172

Sindacatura, 127

Siracusa, 92

Smollet, Tobias, 27

Il Socrate Immaginario, 58

Spaccaforno, Marquis of, 91, 128

Spain, 8, 11, 27, 52–53, 67–68, 79, 185, 190–192

Sperlinga, Duke of, 135

Lo Spione italiano, 48, 207n.30, 208n.7

Stigliano, Viceroy, 68, 97, 119

Supremo Magistrato di Commercio, 27, 37, 53

Table of judges, 137, 138

Tanucci, Marquis: appointment of Caracciolo as Viceroy, 64–68; Caracciolo as ambassador in London, 20–21, 28–32, 33–35, 36, 41; Caracciolo as ambassador in Paris, 42, 49–54, 57; Caracciolo as diplomat, 6–8,

13–15, 17–20; Caracciolo as prime minister, 185, 186, 198, 201; Caracciolo as Viceroy, 77, 78, 79, 95, 113, 125, 181; correspondence with Caracciolo, 8, 14–16, 18–21, 24, 28–29, 31, 33–35, 42, 49

Taxation, 8, 14–15, 64, 74–75, 84, 87, 89–93, 95, 109, 125, 129–131, 140–141, 146–154, 156–157, 165, 168, 200, 204

Textile industry, 14, 26, 36–38, 83

Torcia, Michele, 41

Torremuzza, Prince of, 179

Trabia, Prince of, 154, 164

Trade, 9, 26–32, 33–35, 36–38

Trade guilds, 65, 96, 97, 107, 133, 134

Trapani, 33, 108, 128

Treaties of commerce, 26–27, 189, 190

Treaty of Aix-la-Chapelle, 8, 11, 13, 18

Treaty of Madrid, 27, 31, 32

Treaty of Paris, 20

Tribunale del Real Patrimonio, 171, 200

Tunisia, 28, 190

Turgot, Anne Robert Jacques, 48, 56, 57, 165

Turin, 11–22, 189

Turkey, 190, 194

Two Sicilies *see* Kingdom of the Two Sicilies

Ugo, Vincenzo, 117

Universities, 4, 95, 123, 179, 193, 200, 205

University of Palermo, 4, 123, 179

Urban II, Pope, 73, 105

Valguarnera, Giuseppe, 117
Vatican, 195, 197, 198
Vella, Abbot, 179, 193
Ventimiglia di Geraci, house of,
    161, 162
Ventimiglia, Grand Inquisitor,
    120
Verri, Paolo, 40
Verri, Pietro, 40
Vicaria court, 6, 186
Vicaria prison, 96
Victor, King, 17
Vienna, 66, 67, 68, 185
Villabianca, Francesco Maria
    Emmanuele Gaetani, Marquis di,

86, 101–102, 105, 107, 111, 113,
    115–117, 122, 128–129, 131,
    134, 138–139, 146, 148, 150, 158,
    161–162, 167, 173, 175,
    179–180, 212n.1
Villafranca, Prince of, 158, 159
Villarosa, Duke of, 201
Vittorio, King, 16
Vogli, Marc'Antonio, 179
Volentes, 75, 76, 78, 201
Voltaire, 48, 56, 67
Voto, 156, 165

Water reforms, 139–140
West Indies, 32, 33, 55